How Things Are Made

Trees to Paper

By Inez Snyder

New Lenox
Public Library District
120 Veterans Parkway
New Lenox, Illinois 60451

Children's Press®
A Division of Scholastic Inc.
New York / Toronto / London / Auckland / Sydney
Mexico City / New Delhi / Hong Kong
Danbury, Connecticut

Photo Credits: Cover © Premium Stock/Corbis; p. 5, 21 (upper left) © Stuart Westmorland/
Corbis; p. 7 © Kevin Fleming/Corbis; p. 9, 21 (upper right) © David Lees/Corbis; p. 11 © Morton
Beebe/Corbis; p. 13, 15, 17, 21(lower left and lower right) © Ecoscene/Corbis; p. 19 © Nancy
Sheehan/Index Stock Imagery, Inc.
Contributing Editor: Jennifer Silate
Book Design: Mindy Liu

Library of Congress Cataloging-in-Publication Data

Snyder, Inez.
    Trees to paper / by Inez Snyder.
    p. cm. — (How things are made)
    Summary: Simple words and photographs show the steps involved in making
paper.
    ISBN 0-516-24264-4 (lib. bdg.) — ISBN 0-516-24356-X (pbk.)
    1. Papermaking—Juvenile literature. [1. Papermaking.] I. Title. II. Series.

TS1105.5 .S68 2003
676—dc21
                        3 1984 00239 2940   2002007208

Contents

Paper is made from trees.

The wood from the trees is cut into small **pieces**.

Water and **chemicals** are added to the wood.

This **mixture** is called **pulp**.

9

The pulp is put
into **machines**.

The pulp is wet.

Then, the pulp is **spread** out flat on a machine.

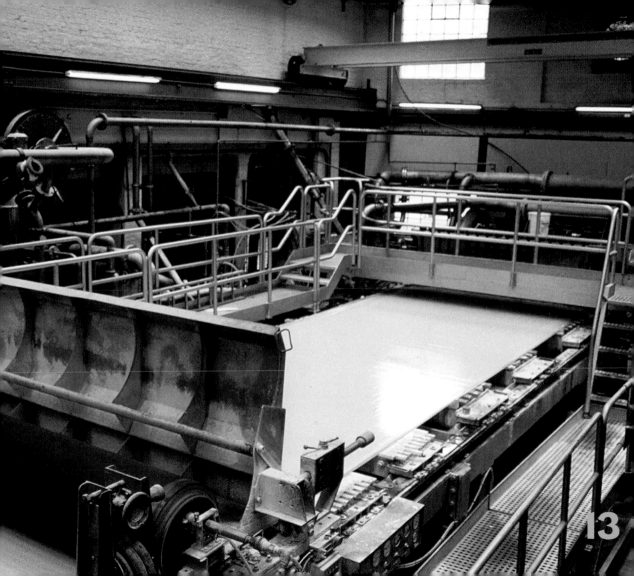

13

The pulp goes through many machines.

This machine dries the pulp.

The dry pulp is paper.

This machine cuts the paper into different sizes.

Paper is used for many things.

We write and draw on paper.

Many things must be done to make paper from trees.

New Words

chemicals (**kem**-uh-kuhlz) substances used
   in chemistry
machines (muh-**sheenz**) equipment with moving
   parts that are used to do a job
mixture (**miks**-chur) something that is made up of
   different things mixed together
pieces (**peess**-uhz) bits of something larger
pulp (**puhlp**) a soft, wet mixture of wood
   and chemicals
spread (**spred**) to unfold or stretch out

To Find Out More

Books
Paper
by Annabelle Dixon
Garrett Educational

Papermaking for Kids
by Beth Wilkinson
Gibbs Smith, Publisher

Web Site
Paper University
http://www.tappi.org/paperu
Play fun games and learn about paper and how it is made
on this Web site.

Index

About the Author

Inez Snyder writes and edits children's books. She also enjoys painting and cooking for her family.

Reading Consultants

Kris Flynn, Coordinator, Small School District Literacy, The San Diego County Office of Education

Shelly Forys, Certified Reading Recovery Specialist, W.J. Zahnow Elementary School, Waterloo, IL

Sue McAdams, Former President of the North Texas Reading Council of the IRA, and Early Literacy Consultant, Dallas, TX

JESUS
UNLEASHED

OTHER BOOKS BY JOHN MACARTHUR

JESUS UNLEASHED

A NEW VISION OF THE BOLD CONFRONTATIONS OF CHRIST AND WHY THEY MATTER

JOHN MACARTHUR

NELSON
BOOKS

An Imprint of Thomas Nelson

Jesus Unleashed

© 2021 John MacArthur

Derived from material previously published in *The Jesus You Can't Ignore.*

Published in Nashville, Tennessee, by Nelson Books, an imprint of Thomas Nelson. Nelson Books and Thomas Nelson are registered trademarks of HarperCollins Christian Publishing, Inc.

Thomas Nelson titles may be purchased in bulk for educational, business, fundraising, or sales promotional use. For information, please e-mail SpecialMarkets@ThomasNelson.com.

Unless otherwise noted, Scripture quotations marked NKJV are taken from the New King James Version®. Copyright © 1982 by Thomas Nelson. Used by permission. All rights reserved.

Scripture quotations marked NASB are taken from the New American Standard Bible® (NASB). Copyright © 1960, 1971, 1977, 1995, 2020 by The Lockman Foundation. Used by permission. www.lockman.org

Scripture quotations marked KJV are taken from the King James Version of the Bible.

Wherever words are italicized in Scripture quotations, the italics have been added for emphasis.

Any internet addresses, phone numbers, or company or product information printed in this book are offered as a resource and are not intended in any way to be or to imply an endorsement by Thomas Nelson, nor does Thomas Nelson vouch for the existence, content, or services of these sites, phone numbers, companies, or products beyond the life of this book.

ISBN 978-0-7852-4297-0

Printed in the United States of America

21 22 23 24 25 LSC 10 9 8 7 6 5 4 3 2 1

CONTENTS

PREFACE

Try to imagine a Bible teacher so devoted to the truth that he never misses an opportunity to confront false teachers and refute their errors. He exposes and rebukes religious hypocrisy wherever he sees it. He is not an insider as far as the current power structure is concerned; he doesn't have any of the customary credentials. But advanced degrees and exalted titles do not intimidate him. He is, if anything, more forthright and severe with the priestly elite than with unschooled lay people. And he never shies away from controversy.

Someone like that would be despised and rejected by today's evangelicals—especially by the movement's most influential leaders. They would do their best to muzzle him and check his influence, even if they agreed with his views. Because in this postmodern era of tolerance and diversity, agreeability is deemed a higher virtue than faithfulness in the pursuit of biblical truth.

But the person in the above description is Jesus. He was deliberately provocative. He was passionate for the truth and therefore fiercely indignant against the religious hypocrisy and unbiblical doctrine of false teachers—especially the leading Pharisees. *They* wore a genteel, scholarly disguise and demanded His respect. *He* was relentlessly harsh with them.

It seems most evangelicals in the current generation would prefer a more domesticated, deferential Messiah. They want Him to be passive, polite, politically correct, and always pleasant. Any suggestion that our Lord might ever be angry or argumentative poses a severe challenge to the image they have created in their imaginations. They must at all costs keep Jesus subdued and make Him safe.

But Scripture stresses that Jesus spoke and taught "as one having authority" (Matthew 7:29)—unrestrained, assertive, and at times angry.

It's true that Jesus is merciful, gracious, and sympathetic to our weaknesses (Hebrews 4:15). "He can have compassion on those who are ignorant and going astray, since he himself is also subject to weakness" (5:2). He is portrayed in prophetic imagery as a lamb, and also as a tender shepherd.

But He is also depicted in Scripture as a lion. He is "the Lion of the tribe of Judah" (Revelation 5:5). And He is not to be muzzled or declawed. It is pure blasphemy to imagine that toning Him down would somehow improve His character, make Him seem "nicer," or elevate His glory.

My objective in this book is to highlight the boldness and power of Jesus by examining the intensity of His interaction with the Pharisees—listening as He speaks for Himself, without attempting to soften or censor anything. "See then the kindness *and* severity of God" (Romans 11:22 NASB).

As C. S. Lewis wrote about Aslan (the messiah figure in *The Chronicles of Narnia*), "He isn't safe. But he's good."

INTRODUCTION

ac•a•dem•ic (ak e-DEM ik) *adj*. 1. abstract,
speculative, or conjectural with very little practical
significance. 2. pertaining to scholars and
institutions of higher learning rather than to lay
people or children. 3. of interest as an intellectual
curiosity, but not particularly useful in real-world
applications. 4. provoking curiosity and analysis
rather than passion or devotion. 5. pedantic,
casuistical; good for making a display of erudition
but otherwise trivial. 6. belonging to that realm
of scholastic theory and intellectual inquiry where
certainty is always inappropriate. 7. not worth
getting agitated about.

Spiritual truth is not "academic" by any of the above definitions.
What you believe about God is the most important feature
of your whole worldview. It will color how you think about
everything else—especially how you prioritize values, how you
determine right and wrong, and what you think of your own
place in the universe. That in turn will surely determine how
you act.

The practical effects of apathy or unbelief are as potent as
those of heartfelt devotion—only in the opposite direction. An

atheist's private life will inevitably become a living demonstration of the evils of unbelief. To whatever degree some atheists seek to maintain a public veneer of virtue and respectability—as well as when they themselves make moral judgments about others—they are walking contradictions. What possible "virtue" could there be in an accidental universe with no Lawgiver and no Judge?

People who profess faith in the Almighty but refuse to think seriously about Him are also living illustrations of this same principle. In fact, the hypocrisy of a superficially religious person has potentially even more sinister implications than outright atheism, because of its deceptiveness.

It is the height of irrationality and arrogance to call Christ Lord with the lips while defying Him with one's life. Yet that is precisely how multitudes live (Luke 6:46). Such people are even more preposterous examples of self-contradiction than the atheist who imagines he can deny the Source of all that's good and yet somehow be "good" himself. But the hypocrite is not only more *irrational*; he is also more *contemptible* than the out-and-out atheist, because he is actually doing gross violence to the truth while pretending to believe it. Nothing is more completely diabolical. Satan is the master hypocrite, disguising himself so that he appears good rather than evil. He "transforms himself into an angel of light. Therefore it is no great thing if his ministers also transform themselves into ministers of righteousness, whose end will be according to their works" (2 Corinthians 11:14–15).

It is no accident, then, that Jesus' harshest words were reserved for institutionalized religious hypocrisy. He waged a very aggressive public controversy against the chief hypocrites of His era. That conflict began almost as soon as He entered public ministry and continued relentlessly until the day He was crucified. In fact, it was the main reason they conspired to crucify Him.

His campaign against hypocrisy is a prominent, if not dominant, emphasis in all four gospels. Jesus never suffered professional hypocrites or false teachers gladly. He never shied away from conflict. He never softened His message to please genteel tastes or priggish scruples. He never suppressed any truth in order to accommodate someone's artificial notion of dignity. He never bowed to the intimidation of scholars or paid homage to their institutions.

And He never, never, never treated the vital distinction between truth and error as a merely academic question.

———————————

I never could believe in the Jesus Christ of some people, for the Christ in whom they believe is simply full of affectionateness and gentleness, whereas I believe there never was a more splendid specimen of manhood, even its sternness, than the Saviour; and the very lips which declared that He would not break a bruised reed uttered the most terrible anathemas upon the Pharisees.

—Charles H. Spurgeon

One

WHEN IT'S WRONG TO BE "NICE"

Then, in the hearing of all the people, He said to His disciples, "Beware of the scribes . . ."
LUKE 20:45–46

Jesus' way of dealing with sinners was normally marked by such extreme tenderness that He earned a derisive moniker from His critics: "Friend of Sinners" (Matthew 11:19). When He encountered even the grossest of moral lepers (ranging from a woman living in adultery in John 4:7–29 to a man infested with a whole legion of demons in Luke 8:27–39), Jesus always ministered to them with remarkable benevolence—without delivering any scolding lectures or sharp rebukes. Invariably, when such people came to Him, they were already broken, humbled, and fed up with the life of sin. He eagerly granted such people forgiveness, healing, and full fellowship with Him on the basis of their faith alone (cf. Luke 7:50; 17:19).

The one class of sinners Jesus consistently dealt with sternly were the professional hypocrites—religious phonies, false teachers, and self-righteous peddlers of plastic piety—the scribes, lawyers, Sadducees, and Pharisees. These were the religious leaders in Israel—spiritual "rulers" (to use a term Scripture often applies to them). They were the despotic gate-keepers of religious tradition. They cared more for custom and convention than they did for the truth. Almost every time they appear in the gospel accounts, they are concerned mainly with keeping up appearances and holding on to their power. Any thought they might have had for authentic godliness always took a back seat to more academic, pragmatic, or self-serving matters. They were the quintessential religious hypocrites.

The Sanhedrin and the Sadducees

The ruling power these men possessed was derived from a large council based in Jerusalem, consisting of seventy-one promi-nent religious authorities, collectively known as the *Sanhedrin*. Council members included the high priest and seventy lead-ing priests and religious scholars. (The number was derived from Moses' appointment of seventy advisors to assist him in Numbers 11:16.) The Sanhedrin had ultimate authority over Israel in all religious and spiritual matters (and thus even in some civil affairs).

The gospel accounts of Christ's crucifixion refer about a dozen times to the Sanhedrin as "the chief priests, the scribes, and the elders" (e.g., Matthew 26:3; Luke 20:1). The high priest presided over the full council, of course. The *chief priests* were the ranking aristocracy of the high-priestly line. (Some of them were men who had already served as high priest at one time or another; others were in line to serve a term in that office.) Virtually all the chief priests were also Sadducees.

The *elders* were key leaders and influential members of important families outside the high-priestly line—and they too were predominantly Sadducees. The *scribes* were the scholars, not necessarily of noble birth like the chief priests and elders, but men who were distinguished mainly because of their expertise in scholarship and their encyclopedic knowledge of Jewish law and tradition. Their group was dominated by Pharisees.

So the council consisted of a blend of Pharisees and Sadducees, and those were rival parties. Although Sadducees were vastly outnumbered by Pharisees in the culture at large, the Sadducees nevertheless maintained a sizable majority in the Sanhedrin, and they held on to the reins of power tightly. The status of their priestly birthright in effect trumped the Pharisees' scholarly clout, because the Pharisees were such devoted traditionalists that they bowed to the authority of the high-priestly line—even though they strongly disagreed with practically everything that made the Sadducees' belief system distinctive.

For example, the Sadducees questioned the immortality of the human soul—denying both the resurrection of the body (Matthew 22:23), and the existence of the spirit world (Acts 23:8). The Sadducean party also rejected the Pharisees' emphasis on oral traditions—going about as far as they could in the opposite direction. In fact, the Sadducees stressed the Pentateuch (the five books of Moses) almost to the exclusion of the rest of the Old Testament. As a result, the powerful messianic expectation that pervaded the teaching of the Pharisees was almost completely missing from the Sadducees' worldview.

In most respects, the Sadducees were classic theological liberals. Their skepticism with regard to heaven, angels, and the afterlife automatically made them worldly minded and power hungry. They were much more interested in (and skilled at) the *politics* of Judaism than they were devoted to the religion itself.

Meet the Pharisees

Nevertheless, it was the Pharisees, not the more doctrinally aberrant Sadducees, who became the main figures of public opposition to Jesus in all four New Testament gospel accounts. Their teaching dominated and epitomized the religion of first-century Israel.

The word *Pharisee* is most likely based on a Hebrew root meaning "separate." Pharisees had an ostentatious way of trying to keep themselves separate from everything that had any connotation of ceremonial defilement. Their obsession with the external badges of piety was their most prominent feature, and they wore it on their sleeves—literally. They used the broadest possible leather straps to bind phylacteries on their arms and foreheads. (Phylacteries were leather boxes containing bits of parchment inscribed with verses from the Hebrew Scriptures.) They also lengthened the tassels on their garments (see Deuteronomy 22:12) in order to make their public display of religious devotion as conspicuous as possible. Thus they had taken a symbol that was meant to be a reminder to themselves (Numbers 15:38–39) and turned it into an advertisement of their self-righteousness, in order to gain the attention of others.

The Pharisees' influence was so profound in early first-century Jewish life that even the Pharisees' theological adversaries, the Sadducees, had to conform to the Pharisees' style of prayer and ceremonialism in their public behavior, or else popular opinion would not have tolerated them.

So the Pharisees' clout was palpable in Israel's daily life during Jesus' lifetime—especially with regard to issues of public piety like Sabbath regulations, ritual washings, dietary restrictions, and other issues of ceremonial purity. These things became the emblems of the Pharisees' influence, and they made it their business to try to enforce their customs on everyone in the culture—even though many of their traditions had no basis whatsoever in Scripture. Most of their conflicts with Jesus centered on precisely those issues, and from the very start of His public ministry, the Pharisees set themselves against Him with the fiercest kind of opposition.

There were some exceptional Pharisees, of course. Nicodemus was a prominent "ruler of the Jews" (John 3:1). Another council member, Joseph of Arimathea (Mark 15:43; Luke 23:50), became a disciple of Christ "secretly, for fear of the Jews" (John 19:38).

As a rule, however, Jesus' interactions with the Pharisees, Sadducees, scribes, and leading priests were marked by acrimony, not tenderness. He rebuked them publicly and to their faces. He repeatedly said harsh things *about* them in His sermons and public discourses. He warned His followers to beware of their deadly influence. He consistently employed stronger language in His denunciations of the Pharisees than He ever used against the pagan Roman authorities or their occupying armies.

That constant attack absolutely infuriated the Pharisees. They gladly would have embraced any messiah who opposed the Roman occupation of Israel and affirmed their pharisaical traditions. Jesus, however, spoke not a word against Caesar while treating the entire religious aristocracy of Israel as if they were more dangerous tyrants than Caesar himself.

Indeed, they were. In spiritual terms, the self-righteousness and religious traditionalism of the Pharisees represented a more clear and present danger to the vital health of the nation than the tightening political vise that had already been clamped on Israel by Caesar and his occupying armies. That is saying quite a lot, given the fact that in less than half a century Roman armies would completely lay waste to Jerusalem and drive Israel's population into a far-flung exile (the Diaspora) from which the Jewish people have not fully emerged even today.

But as profound and far-reaching as the holocaust of AD 70 was for the Jewish nation, a far greater calamity was looming in the institutionalized self-righteousness of the Pharisees' brand of religion—especially their preference for human traditions over the Word of God. That led to a *spiritual* disaster of eternal and infinite proportions, because most Israelites in that generation rejected their true Messiah—and multitudes of their descendants have continued the relentless pursuit of religious tradition for almost two full millennia, many refusing to give any serious consideration to the claims of Christ as God's Messiah.

The Pharisees' legalistic system was in effect a steamroller paving the way for that tragedy. The apostle Paul (a converted Pharisee himself) was describing pharisaical religion to a T in Romans 10:2–3, when he lamented the unbelief of Israel: "I bear them witness that they have a zeal for God, but not according to knowledge. For they being ignorant of God's righteousness, and seeking to establish their own righteousness, have not submitted to the righteousness of God."

The Pharisees did indeed have a kind of zeal for God. They were genuine experts when it came to knowing the *words* of Scripture. They were also fastidious in their observance of the law's tiniest external details. If they purchased seeds for their herb gardens, for example, they would meticulously count the grains in each packet and measure out a tithe (Matthew 23:23).

From a human perspective, those things all had the appearance of profound devotion to God. Looked at in that way, the Pharisees might have been thought the *least* likely men of their generation to become Messiah's worst enemies. They were profoundly religious, not careless or profane. They certainly weren't avowed atheists openly undermining people's faith in God's Word. They promoted piety, not licentiousness. They advocated zeal, rigor, and abstinence—not worldliness and indifference to spiritual things. They championed Judaism, not the sort of pagan syncretism their Samaritan neighbors and so many earlier generations of Israelites had dabbled in. Their religion was their whole life.

It even took precedence over God Himself.

And therein lay the problem. The Pharisees had devised a slick disguise, concealing their self-righteousness and hypocrisy under a veneer of religious zeal. They were careful to maintain the appearance of—but not the reality of—sincere devotion to God. More than that, they had so thoroughly blended their manmade religious traditions with the revealed truth of God that they themselves could not even tell the difference anymore. Despite all their studied expertise in the unique variety of Old Testament scholarship they promoted, they insisted on viewing Scripture through the lens of human tradition. Tradition therefore became their primary authority. There was no way for Scripture to correct their *faulty* traditions. The Pharisees thus became the chief architects of a corrupted brand of cultural and traditional (but not truly biblical) Judaism.

The Pharisees who blindly followed the party line were the worst kind of wolves in sheep's clothing—corrupt rabbis wearing the wool robes of a prophet and devouring the sheep of the Lord's flock under the cover of that disguise. They were in fact determined rebels against God and His Anointed One, even though they covered themselves with such a cloying, pretentious display of external piety. And when confronted with liberating biblical truth, they stubbornly carried on being shills for legalism.

No wonder Jesus dealt so sternly with them.

The Evil of False Religion

Men and women who lack a biblical worldview tend to think of religion as the noblest expression of the human character. Popular opinion in the world at large has generally regarded religion as something inherently admirable, honorable, and beneficial.

In reality, no other field of the humanities—philosophy, literature, the arts, or whatever—holds quite as much potential for mischief as religion. Nothing is more thoroughly evil than *false* religion, and the more false teachers try to cloak themselves in the robes of biblical truth, the more truly Satanic they are.

Nevertheless, benign-looking, suavely religious emissaries of Satan are ordinary, not extraordinary. Redemptive history is full of them, and the Bible continually warns about such false teachers—savage wolves in sheep's clothing, "false apostles, deceitful workers, transforming themselves into apostles of Christ" (2 Corinthians 11:13). Indeed, nothing is more thoroughly diabolical, and we are warned repeatedly not to take false teaching lightly because of its close resemblance to the truth.

Never were false teachers more aggressive than during the earthly ministry of the Lord Jesus Christ. It was as if all hell amassed its heaviest assault ever against Him during those three years. And the fiercest opposition to Christ came from the most respected leaders of society's religious sector. It wasn't from the culture's criminal underworld or its secular underclass. It wasn't from society's outcasts—the tax collectors, lowlifes, thugs, prostitutes, and thieves. Instead, the chief emissaries and agents of Satan were the most devout, the most sanctimonious, and the most respected religious leaders in all of Israel—led in that effort by the very strictest of all their major sects, the Pharisees.

Dances with Wolves

Any literal shepherd tasked with feeding and leading a flock of lambs would be thought deranged if he regarded wolves as potential pets to be domesticated and amalgamated into the fold. Suppose he actively sought and tried to befriend young wolves, presuming he could teach them to mingle with his sheep—*insisting* against all wise counsel that his experiment might succeed, and if it does, the wolves will acquire the sheep's gentleness and the sheep will learn things from the wolves too.

Such a shepherd would be worse than useless; he himself would pose an extreme danger to the flock.

Nearly as bad would be a shepherd whose vision is myopic. He has never seen a wolf clearly with his own eyes. He therefore believes the threat of wolves is grossly exaggerated. Even though his sheep keep disappearing or getting torn to shreds by *something,* he refuses to believe it is wolves that are harming his flock. He declares that he is tired of hearing shrill wolf-warnings from others. He begins telling the story of "The Boy Who Cried Wolf" to everyone who will listen. Finally concluding that other people's "negativity" toward wolves poses a greater danger to his flock than the wolves themselves, he takes out his reed and plays a gentle tune to lull the lambs to sleep.

Then, of course, there is the "hireling, he who is not the shepherd, one who does not own the sheep." He "sees the wolf coming and leaves the sheep and flees; and the wolf catches the sheep and scatters them. The hireling flees because he is a hireling and does not care about the sheep" (John 10:12–13).

One key lesson we can learn from the example of Jesus is that even the kindest, gentlest shepherd will wage war against the wolves who try to sneak into the flock disguised in sheep's clothing—because a true shepherd *does* care about his sheep.

Was Jesus Always "Nice"?

The Great Shepherd Himself was never far from open controversy with the most conspicuously religious inhabitants in all of Israel. Almost every chapter of the Gospels makes some reference to His running battle with the chief hypocrites of His day, and He made no effort whatsoever to be winsome in His encounters with them.

Jesus' public ministry was barely underway when He invaded what they thought was their turf—the temple grounds in Jerusalem—and went on a righteous rampage against their mercenary control of Israel's worship. He did the same thing again during the final week before His crucifixion, immediately after His triumphal entry into the city. One of His last major public discourses was the solemn pronunciation of seven woes against the scribes and Pharisees. These were formal curses against them. That sermon was the farthest thing from a friendly dialogue. Matthew's record of it fills an entire chapter (Matthew 23), and as noted earlier, it is entirely devoid of any positive or encouraging word for the Pharisees and their followers. Luke distills and summarizes the entire message in three short verses: "Then, in the hearing of all the people, He said to His disciples, 'Beware of the scribes, who desire to go around in long robes, love greetings in the marketplaces, the best seats in the synagogues, and the best places at feasts, who devour widows' houses, and for a pretense make long prayers. These will receive greater condemnation'" (Luke 20:45–47).

That is a perfect summary of Jesus' dealings with the Pharisees. It is a blistering denunciation—a candid diatribe about the seriousness of their error. There is no conversation, no collegiality, no dialogue, and no cooperation. Only confrontation, condemnation, and (as Matthew records) curses against them.

Jesus' compassion is certainly evident in two facts that bracket this declamation. First, Luke says that as He drew near the city and observed its full panorama for this final time, He paused and wept over it (19:41–44). And second, Matthew records a similar lament at the end of the seven woes (23:37). So we can be absolutely certain that as Jesus delivered this diatribe, His heart was full of compassion.

Yet that compassion is directed at the victims of the false teaching, not the false teachers themselves. There is no hint of sympathy, no proposal of clemency, no trace of kindness, no effort on Jesus' part to be "nice" toward the Pharisees. Indeed, with these words Jesus formally and resoundingly pronounced their doom and then held them up publicly as a warning to others.

Let's turn back to the very beginning of Jesus' ministry and observe how this hostility between Him and the Pharisees began and how it developed. I think many readers will be surprised to discover that it was Jesus who fired the first shot. And it was a shockingly powerful broadside.

The stern and holy Christ, the indignant, mighty Messiah, the Messenger of the Covenant of whom it is written: "He shall purify the sons of Levi, and purge them as gold and silver, that they may offer unto the Lord an offering of righteousness," is not agreeable to those who want only a soft and sweet Christ. [What we see instead is] the fiery zeal of Jesus which came with such sudden and tremendous effectiveness that before this unknown man, who had no further authority than his own person and word, this crowd of traders and changers, who thought they were fully within their rights when conducting their business in the Temple court, fled pellmell like a lot of naughty boys.
—R. C. H. Lenski

Two

TWO PASSOVERS

They found Him in the temple, sitting in the midst of the teachers, both listening to them and asking them questions.
LUKE 2:46

When He had made a whip of cords, He drove them all out of the temple.
JOHN 2:15

Jesus' earliest recorded encounter with Jerusalem's leading rabbis was the mildest, most benign of all His recorded face-to-face meetings with them. It occurred when He was still a boy of twelve, visiting Jerusalem with His parents for the Passover feast. "His parents went to Jerusalem every year at the Feast of the Passover. And when He was twelve years old, they went up to Jerusalem according to the custom of the feast" (Luke 2:41–42). Of all the gospel writers, Luke alone has anything to say about Jesus' childhood or adolescence, and this is the only episode Luke recorded from the birth of Jesus until His baptism.

The day after Passover each year began a weeklong celebration known as the Feast of Unleavened Bread (Leviticus 23:6–8). Combined, these two holidays spanned eight full days. During that week, all of Jerusalem would be jammed with pilgrims who came to offer sacrifices, partake of the feasts, and participate in other festivities.

Passover in Jerusalem—Scene One

At twelve in that culture, Jesus was on the doorstep of manhood. The following year He would be a *bar mitzvah*—a son of the commandment. He would then be formally regarded as an adult, personally accountable to the law, and eligible to take part publicly in Jewish worship. Until then, however, He was still a child—and not only in the eyes of His culture. He was a real child in every sense undergoing all the normal processes of biological, mental, and social development. In other words, Jesus as a child was not some kind of paranormal prodigy. The gospel record makes this inescapably clear.

In fact, this brief window into His childhood is one of the Bible's most vivid portrayals of Christ in His full humanity. What we see in Luke 2 is a very normal boy with true-to-life parents.

Joseph and Mary went annually to Jerusalem to celebrate Passover (v. 41). But it is likely that Luke 2 is describing Jesus' first-ever Passover in Jerusalem. It was customary for boys in their last year of childhood to experience their first feast at the temple. The preparation for *bar mitzvah* required careful instruction in the law, including familiarity with Jewish customs, rituals, feasts, and sacrifices. The Passover week afforded an intensive initiation into all of these, so it was common for boys in their final year of childhood to have the privilege of accompanying their parents to Jerusalem for that week of celebration.

Luke says nothing about the actual Passover celebration or the Feast of Unleavened Bread, but he picks up the story when it was time for the family to return to Galilee:

> When they had finished the days, as they returned, the Boy Jesus lingered behind in Jerusalem. And Joseph and His mother did not know it; but supposing Him to have been in the company, they went a day's journey, and sought Him among their relatives and acquaintances. So when they did not find Him, they returned to Jerusalem, seeking Him.
>
> **(Luke 2:43–45)**

Jesus' separation from His parents was rooted in a very simple misunderstanding on their part. The gospel account by no means suggests that Jesus was being mischievous or rebellious. He was simply engrossed in the goings-on at the temple—the very thing He was there to participate in. On the day they were scheduled to depart, however, Jesus' parents were preoccupied with preparations for the journey home. When they left, He lingered—not out of disrespect or defiance, but simply because (like all children) He was utterly absorbed in something that had arrested His attention. His true humanness never shows more clearly than it does in this account.

Because so many pilgrims descended on Jerusalem during that week, all the roads and inns would be jammed, and large numbers of people from each community would travel to and from the feast together. From a town the size of Nazareth, there may have been a hundred or more people in Jesus' parents' party, some walking, some riding slow beasts of burden. A band that large would likely stretch over a mile's distance, and the women generally traveled in a group or several small groups together, rather than being spread out among the men.

So it is easy to understand how this confusion arose. Mary and Joseph no doubt each presumed Jesus was with the other parent. He certainly would not have been a mischief-prone child, so neither parent gave any thought to investigating His whereabouts until the end of the first day's travel, when they suddenly discovered He was not with the group at all. They immediately returned and frantically scoured all of Jerusalem, checking and rechecking all the places they had been with Him.

Except, perhaps, the most obvious place: "Now so it was that after three days they found Him in the temple, sitting in the midst of the teachers, both listening to them and asking them questions. And all who heard Him were astonished at His understanding and answers" (vv. 46–47).

This is a unique picture of Jesus, seated among Israel's leading rabbis, politely listening to them, asking questions, and amazing them with His comprehension and discernment. Still a child in every sense, He was already the most amazing student they had ever had the privilege to teach. He had evidently kept these teachers fully engaged for three days. Luke says Jesus was listening and asking questions, and what amazed these tutors was His grasp of the information they were giving Him and His answers (v. 47). So they were obviously quizzing Him as they went, and they were astonished at both His attention span and His ability to perceive spiritual truth.

It would have been an amazing lesson to eavesdrop on, and it is the only time in all the gospel accounts where we see Jesus sitting at anyone's feet to learn. No doubt throughout His childhood He *did* have other teachers as well, and Luke seems to acknowledge this in his description of how Jesus matured (v. 52), but Luke 2:46 remains the only brief window into Jesus' student career that we are given anywhere in Scripture. And it is the only record in all the gospels of an extended friendly exchange between Jesus and any group of leading rabbis.

The lesson came to a rather abrupt halt when Joseph and Mary finally found Jesus. Their anxiety and exasperation are certainly easy to understand from any parent's point of view: "When they saw Him, they were amazed; and His mother said to Him, 'Son, why have You done this to us? Look, Your father and I have sought You anxiously'" (v. 48).

This was probably not the first time—and it certainly would not be the last—that Jesus' innocent motives would be misunderstood and misconstrued. Nor should His reply to Joseph and Mary be read as an insolent retort. He was truly amazed that they hadn't known exactly where to look for Him. "He said to them, 'Why did you seek Me? Did you not know that I must be about My Father's business?'" (v. 49).

Mary, of course, was referring to Joseph when she said, "your father." Jesus, however, was calling God "My Father." (Plainly Jesus already had a clear sense of who He was and where His true accountability lay.) But at the moment, Jesus' parents were so overwhelmed with relief to have found Him, so amazed to find Him at the feet of these prominent rabbis, and so fatigued from the whole ordeal that "they did not understand the statement which He spoke to them" (v. 50).

Passover in Jerusalem—Scene Two

Fast forward more than fifteen years. Jesus is now a fully mature adult about thirty years old, and He is back in Jerusalem for another Passover. "Now the Passover of the Jews was at hand, and Jesus went up to Jerusalem" (John 2:13). His public ministry will last a little more than three years total, and thus it spans four Passovers. His reputation will quickly begin to spread during this first Passover week, and His crucifixion will occur on Passover Day exactly three years later.

Scripture gives us no information whatsoever about Jesus' life after the end of Luke 2 until He comes to be baptized in the Jordan River. So John is recording the very earliest close-up look at Jesus in a public, urban context. In fact, this Passover is really the first major public event of our Lord's ministry. Although Jesus will work and live mostly in Galilee, He chooses the biggest event of the year in Jerusalem to make His public debut. As we see from the narrative that unfolds, Jesus makes no attempt to come across as "positive" before provoking a confrontation:

> He found in the temple those who sold oxen and sheep and doves, and the money changers doing business. When He had made a whip of cords, He drove them all out of the temple, with the sheep and the oxen, and poured out the changers' money and overturned the tables. And He said to those who sold doves, "Take these things away! Do not make My Father's house a house of merchandise!"
>
> (vv. 14–16)

Jerusalem was again jammed with pilgrims, not only from all over the land of Israel, but also from Jewish communities throughout the Roman world. The population of the city might more than double during a typical Passover week. Of course, merchants throughout the city profited immensely from the revenue that came in from pilgrims during the holidays.

The temple priests even had their own extremely profitable franchise set up right there on the temple grounds. A portion of the massive outer court (known as the court of the Gentiles) had been turned into a bustling bazaar, filled with licensed animal-merchants and money changers. With multitudes coming to celebrate Passover from all corners of the empire, it was impossible for some of them to bring their own oxen, lambs, or doves for sacrifice. Furthermore, paschal lambs had to be "without blemish, a male of the first year" (Exodus 12:5). Other sacrificial animals likewise all had to be flawless. The law was clear about this: "Whatever has a defect, you shall not offer, for it shall not be acceptable on your behalf" (Leviticus 22:20). Priests would therefore carefully inspect every animal brought to the altar, and if they found a defect, they would pronounce the animal unsuitable. For obvious reasons it would be terribly inconvenient for any family to carry a sacrificial animal more than three day's journey from Galilee only to have it declared unfit for sacrifice. And for many, the journey to Jerusalem was too far even to think of bringing animals for sacrifice along. So the temple merchants sold pre-approved animals—but at a very dear premium.

The money changers' tables were likewise supposed to be a service for pilgrims and worshippers, because offerings to the temple had to be made with Jewish coins. Roman coins had impressions of Caesar (Luke 20:24), which were deemed idolatrous.

The Old Testament prescribed a half-shekel offering from every male twenty years old and older, to be offered with each national census (Exodus 30:13–14). The half-shekel tax was specifically to be used for the maintenance of the temple (v. 16), and by the first century, with Herod's massive rebuilding of the whole temple grounds, this had become an annual donation, required of every devout Hebrew man. A half-shekel coin was roughly equivalent to two days' pay for the average laborer.

Obviously, foreigners needed to exchange their money for authentic half-shekel coins in order to make the donation, and temple authorities appear to have cornered the market for all Hebrew currency exchange in Jerusalem. The result was that they charged a usurious exchange rate for the coins.

Under Old Testament law, Jews were not permitted to charge interest to their own countrymen, whether "on money or food or anything that is lent out at interest" (Deuteronomy 23:19). So a high exchange rate on half-shekel coins was bad enough under any circumstances. But the fact that this was being done with the offerings of worshippers, on the temple grounds, under the temple authorities' oversight and with their encouragement, was positively evil. In effect, temple authorities were housing and profiting from a den of thieves (cf. Mark 11:17)—exploiting the very people they ought to have been ministering to. Such exploitation is what caused Jesus to pronounce the total destruction of the temple (Luke 21:6).

It's not hard to imagine what all this activity did to the ambience of the temple grounds, either. Bleating sheep, bawling oxen, haggling merchants, and indignant pilgrims all raised their voices together amid the miasma of manure from all those animals. It was a hive of noise, dissonance, filth, and pandemonium. It was certainly no atmosphere for worship. It was carnal chaos, the first sight to greet every pilgrim arriving on the temple mount.

Jesus' response actually reflects an amazing degree of patience and deliberation. He carefully, painstakingly braided some cords together to make a whip or a scourge (like a cat-o'-nine-tails). Small cords would be lying around in abundance—cheap strands used to tether the animals.

Jesus' response is amazingly bold, especially when we consider that at this point He was largely unknown, acting out publicly against the most powerful confederacy in Judaism, intruding on their turf (or so *they* thought), and setting Himself against a large number of unscrupulous profitmongers who would not hesitate to use violence against Him.

It seems unlikely that *He* inflicted any physical injury on *them*. A whip of small cords was a common and harmless tool used for driving large animals. (Such a makeshift whip would probably not be capable of inflicting any actual pain on oxen or sheep; it was actually a very mild means of driving them compared to a typical oxgoad.) There's no suggestion that He flogged the merchants or money changers. John 2:15 says, "He drove them all out of the temple, with the sheep and the oxen." Most likely He used the whip to drive the animals, and He used the animals as a motive for the merchants to chase after them. Thus He cleared the area in short order. If any beast or scoundrel offered physical resistance, Scripture doesn't mention it.

He even turned over the money changers' tables and poured their coins onto the ground. There must have been great tumult all around, but in the midst of it, Jesus appears unruffled—fierce in His anger, perhaps, but resolute, single-minded, stoic, and wholly composed. He is the very picture of self-control. This is truly *righteous* indignation, not a violent temper that has gotten out of hand.

The merchants and money changers, by contrast, were instantly sent scrambling. And what bedlam went with them! Animal-merchants frantically chased their sheep and oxen, whose herd instincts would have made the whole evacuation seem very much like a stampede—perhaps down the southern steps, sending waves of pilgrims coming *up* those steps scurrying to get out of the way.

Jesus' complete control of the situation was such that no actual riot broke out. There's no mention of any injury to either man or beast. The most "violent" action described here is the overturning of tables.

John, one of the earliest disciples Jesus called, was undoubtedly present on this day, and he therefore writes this account as an eyewitness. So he describes his own thoughts when He says, "Then His disciples remembered that it was written, 'Zeal for Your house has eaten me up'" (2:17). That is a reference to Psalm 69:9: "Zeal for Your house has eaten me up, and the reproaches of those who reproach You have fallen on me." That verse in turn exactly parallels Psalm 119:139: "My zeal has consumed me, because my enemies have forgotten Your words." Both passages apply perfectly to this incident. Both texts describe a zealous fury that is not the selfish pique of someone who has suffered a personal insult. Instead, it is a deep outrage that comes from the realization that *God* is being dishonored.

Amazingly, the temple authorities did not take Jesus into custody. Clearly, Jesus' point about the defilement of the temple hit its target squarely. The people in the temple courtyard certainly knew they were victims of the swindling merchants' greed. Their sympathies would have been with Jesus. Whatever commotion His actions caused seems to have died down quickly.

This whole episode was obviously a great embarrassment to the Sanhedrin. Jesus exposed the chicanery of their on-site business dealings. He declared them guilty of defiling the temple. He did this openly in broad daylight while the Sanhedrin had home-field advantage. He did not cower and back away when a team of their thugs arrived to challenge Him. And in the end, they were the ones forced to back down, because Jesus' point was too clear and too obvious to refute. If they arrested Him, even on a misdemeanor charge of disturbing the peace, that would necessitate a trial. Witnesses would be deposed. Testimony would be given. And they were already clearly too exposed to want to drag this incident out any further. So it appears they had to let Him walk away.

For those who would prefer a meek, perpetually friendly, sentimental messiah reaching out to other religious leaders and engaging in scholarly dialogue with them instead of challenging them, this may seem to establish a troubling precedent at the very start of His dealings with the Jewish leaders. But by His own avowal, the Prince of Peace is no peacemonger when it comes to hypocrisy and false teaching. "Do not think that I came to bring peace on earth. I did not come to bring peace but a sword" (Matthew 10:34). There was certainly no question

23

about that now in the minds of the Sanhedrin, and most of them utterly hated Him from the start because of the way He humiliated them.

To add irony upon irony, Jesus' only recorded one-on-one encounter with a member of the Sanhedrin would be a secret meeting with a completely different tone and tenor from this one. It will start with an overture of peace—but not from Jesus. The next encounter would be initiated by one of the leading Pharisees, Nicodemus.

There are several things which may help to make the life fair in the eyes of men, but nothing will make it amiable in the eyes of God, unless the heart be changed and renewed. Indeed, all the medicines that can be applied, without the sanctifying work of the Spirit, though they may cover, they can never cure the corruptions and diseases of the soul. . . . Such civil persons go to hell without much disturbance, being asleep in sin, yet not snoring to the disquieting of others; they are so far from being awaked that they are many times praised and commended. Example, custom, and education, may also help a man to make a fair show in the flesh, but not to walk after the Spirit. They may prune and lop sin, but never stub it up by the roots. All that these can do, is to make a man like a grave, green and flourishing on the surface and outside, when within there is nothing but noisomeness and corruption.

—George Swinnock

Three

A MIDNIGHT INTERVIEW

_____

"That which is born of the flesh is flesh, and that which is born of the Spirit is spirit. Do not marvel that I said to you, 'You must be born again.'"
JOHN 3:6–7

From that first pre-Passover run-in with Israel's religious leaders through the end of His earthly ministry, Jesus taught and healed chiefly among the common people, who "heard Him gladly" (Mark 12:37). Scribes, Pharisees, and Sadducees often hung around the edges, watching through critical eyes, occasionally challenging Jesus' teaching or expressing outrage at His refusal to observe all their ceremonial rules. But from this point on, practically all Jesus' recorded encounters with the Pharisees involved conflicts.

A Few Friendly Pharisees

_____

A survey of all the gospels produces very few exceptions to that pattern. But they are worth mentioning.

For example, all three Synoptic Gospels record the raising of Jairus's daughter from the dead (Matthew 9:18–26;

Mark 5:22–43; and Luke 8:41–56). Jairus was a ruler in the Capernaum synagogue, doubtless a disciple of Pharisees—possibly even a Pharisee himself. He is a very rare example of a ruling Jewish leader whom Jesus blessed rather than condemning. Jairus came to Jesus in an hour of desperation, "for he had an only daughter about twelve years of age, and she was dying" (Luke 8:42).

The little girl actually *did* die while Jairus was bringing his request to Jesus (v. 49), and Jesus then raised her from the dead. Jairus, of course, was "astonished" (v. 56)—and he was doubtless moved with the profoundest gratitude. What became of him after that is not recorded, but Jesus' words to him just prior to raising the girl from the dead—"Do not be afraid; only believe" (Mark 5:36)—are nothing if not tender, positive, and reassuring. So it seems fair to infer that Jairus did indeed believe in Christ—one of a small handful of Jewish religious leaders who gave evidence of faith in Jesus while His ministry among the common people was flourishing.

The rich young ruler was likewise a religious official of some sort (see Matthew 19:16–26; Mark 10:17–27; and Luke 18:18–27). He might well have been a Pharisee. After all, one of the Pharisees' characteristic traits was their love of money (Luke 16:14), and that was certainly this young man's besetting sin. But he approached Jesus with a question that certainly *sounded* sincere. Even his greeting rang with authentic respect: "Good Teacher, what shall I do to inherit eternal life?" (Luke 18:18).

Jesus' reply—though not what the young man had hoped to hear—was without any tone of reproach or scolding. In fact, Mark 10:21 expressly tells us that Jesus "loved him," reminding us that Jesus' frequent anger with the Jewish religious leaders, His hatred for their hypocrisy, and His opposition to their errors were by no means inconsistent with authentic love for *them*.

On at least three occasions (all recorded by Luke) Jesus had dinner in the homes of Pharisees (Luke 7:36–50; 11:37–54; 14:1–14). If those events began cordially, they nevertheless all ended with Jesus denouncing the Pharisees' doctrine and practice, so they don't really constitute major deviations from the pattern of Jesus' contentious interactions with Israel's religious leaders.

In fact, the Luke 11 incident ended with Jesus pronouncing a series of woes against the Pharisees and religious lawyers. Luke's closing words in that narrative pretty well describe the flavor of *most* of Jesus' face-to-face conversations with Israel's religious leaders: "As He said these things to them, the scribes and the Pharisees began to assail Him vehemently, and to cross-examine Him about many things, lying in wait for Him, and seeking to catch Him in something He might say, that they might accuse Him" (Luke 11:53–54).

Nick at Night

The account of Nicodemus in John 3 is certainly the most unusual of all Jesus' encounters with Pharisees—and the only significant example of an extended friendly dialogue between Jesus and a Pharisee. In fact, it stands out as the longest personal conversation Jesus had with any religious leader in all the gospel accounts. Notice, however: what makes this meeting so unusual is Nicodemus's response to Jesus. Jesus was no less blunt with Nicodemus than He ever was with any Pharisee. But Nicodemus evidently came to Jesus truly wishing to learn, rather than with the typical pharisaical agenda of self-aggrandizement at Jesus' expense. And the result was a markedly different sort of exchange.

Nicodemus comes on the scene quietly, late at night. Fear of what his fellow council members might think (or do to him) seems to be his motive for coming under cover of darkness.

Nicodemus was clearly intrigued by Christ and showed Him the utmost respect, beginning with an unqualified acknowledgment of Christ's prophetic authority—an affirmation unheard of by any other council member either before or after this. He said, "Rabbi, we know that You are a teacher come from God, for no one can do these signs that You do unless God is with him" (v. 2).

The title "Rabbi" was an expression of honor. Coming from a ruling Pharisee like this, it was a signal that Nicodemus regarded Jesus as an equal. Of course Nicodemus intended that as a great compliment.

An Impossible Demand from Jesus

Jesus' reply was abrupt and to the point, a demonstration of the prophetic authority Nicodemus had just acknowledged: "Truly, truly, I say to you, unless someone is born again he cannot see the kingdom of God" (v. 3 NASB). Ignoring the verbal honor Nicodemus had paid to Him, changing the subject away from His own ability to do miracles, Jesus made a statement that was plainly intended as a remark about Nicodemus's spiritual *inability* and blindness.

It was a breathtaking reply, especially given Nicodemus's stature as a religious leader. Nicodemus was no doubt accustomed to being shown great honor and deference. Jesus' first recorded words to him instead conveyed the clear and deliberate implication that this leading Pharisee was still so far from the kingdom of heaven that he was unable to see it at all. If Nicodemus had been motivated solely by pride, or merely looking for affirmation, he would certainly have been offended by Jesus' reply.

But Nicodemus was clearly being drawn to Christ by the Holy Spirit, because his answer to Jesus was surprisingly unruffled. There's no hint of resentment, no insults directed at Jesus, and no iciness. He continues to show Jesus the respect due a dignified rabbi by asking a series of questions designed to draw the meaning out of Jesus' words—words that must have hit him like a hard slap in the face.

Nicodemus had devoted his life to a rigid observance of the Pharisees' traditions, which he no doubt firmly believed were fully in accord with the law of God. He might have expected a commendation from Jesus for his personal piety. He might have hoped he could help reconcile Jesus and the Sanhedrin after the temple-cleansing incident. That was, after all, Jesus' only public conflict with Israel's religious leaders so far. Nicodemus may well have heard about John the Baptist's advocacy of Jesus. He had obviously heard about (possibly even witnessed) the miracles. In fact, the language Nicodemus used ("*we* know that You are a teacher come from God") suggested that he had discussed Jesus' prophetic credentials with others who agreed that He must be from God. Clearly, Nicodemus approached Jesus with high hopes and eager expectations.

How Jesus' reply must have stunned him! Nicodemus had honored Christ by calling Him Rabbi; Jesus suggested in return that Nicodemus was not even a spiritual beginner yet. He had no part in the kingdom whatsoever. Jesus wasn't being unkind or merely insulting; He was being truthful with a man who desperately needed to hear the truth. Nicodemus's soul was at stake.

"Born again?" Nicodemus did not instantly seem to grasp that Jesus was talking about *regeneration*—the new birth, the spiritual awakening of a dead soul. But it was clear enough that Jesus was calling him to make a whole new start. That was a lot to ask of someone like Nicodemus, who (like any good Pharisee) believed he was accumulating merit with God by a lifetime of careful attention to the law's tiniest ceremonial details. What did Jesus want him to do? Cast all that aside like so much garbage?

That, of course, is precisely how the apostle Paul would later describe his own conversion from Pharisaism in Philippians 3:7–9:

> What things were gain to me, these I have counted loss for Christ. Yet indeed I also count all things loss for the excellence of the knowledge of Christ Jesus my Lord, for whom I have suffered the loss of all things, *and count them as rubbish*, that I may gain Christ and be found in Him, not having my own righteousness, which is from the law, but that which is through faith in Christ, the righteousness which is from God by faith.

Jesus chose the perfect language to convey all that to Nicodemus: "You must be born again" (John 3:7). With that simple expression, Jesus demolished Nicodemus's entire worldview and value system. His Jewish birth and upbringing, his attainments as a leading Pharisee, the care with which he kept himself from ceremonial defilement, the respect he had earned in the eyes of his countrymen, all the merit he thought he had stored up for himself—Jesus reduced it all at once to utter worthlessness. Whatever else Jesus meant, this much was plain: Jesus was demanding that Nicodemus forsake everything he stood for, walk away from everything he had ever done as a Pharisee, abandon hope in everything he ever trusted, and start all over from the beginning.

Nicodemus's reply has often been misunderstood: "How can a man be born when he is old? Can he enter a second time into his mother's womb and be born?" (v. 4). Don't imagine that Nicodemus was so naive as to think Jesus was telling him he literally needed to be physically reborn. Nicodemus must have been a highly skilled teacher himself, or he would not have attained his position. He was clearly a perceptive man—perhaps the most discerning of all the Sanhedrin. So we must give him credit for a modicum of intelligence. His question to Jesus should no more be interpreted as a literal reference to physical birth than Jesus' original remark to him. How well Nicodemus understood Jesus' point isn't spelled out for us in detail, but it is clear that he got the gist of the idea that he needed a whole new start.

Thus his rejoinder to Jesus merely picked up on Jesus' imagery and employed it to show Jesus that he understood the impossibility of what Jesus had prescribed for him. He was a mature man—patriarchal enough in both age and wisdom to serve as one of Israel's chief elders. Membership in the Sanhedrin was an honor not often bestowed on young men. So when Nicodemus asked, "How can a man be born when he is old?" he was pointing out that men his age don't simply decide to start over at the beginning. And when he asked, "Can he enter a second time into his mother's womb and be born?" it's only reasonable to assume he was remarking about the utter impossibility of causing *himself* to be "reborn" in any sense. He certainly understood far more than he is usually given credit for.

A Cryptic Reference from the Old Testament

To anyone who lacked Nicodemus's familiarity with the Old Testament, Jesus' next reply might have only compounded the confusion. Jesus answered, "Most assuredly, I say to you, unless one is born of water and the Spirit, he cannot enter the kingdom of God. That which is born of the flesh is flesh, and that which is born of the Spirit is spirit. Do not marvel that I said to you, 'You must be born again'" (John 3:5–7).

In fact, many Bible students who examine this passage are confused by it. Some have suggested that when Jesus spoke of "water," He was speaking of baptism—and some of them then interpret this to be a statement about the necessity of water baptism as a prerequisite for regeneration. But John's baptism could not have been a means of regeneration, because it signified an already-repentant heart, which is a *fruit* of regeneration. Christian baptism (likewise a symbol, not a means, of regeneration) had not even been instituted yet. The idea of baptism is utterly foreign to this passage.

Some commentators suggest that "water" is a reference to the amniotic fluid that signals the onset of physical birth, and they therefore believe Jesus was describing two distinct births in verse 5—physical birth ("water"), and spiritual birth ("the Spirit"). A closer look, however, shows that verse 5 simply restates verse 3 in different words. Notice the parallelism: "Unless one is *born again,* he cannot see the kingdom of God" (v. 3); and "Unless one is *born of water and the Spirit,* he cannot enter the kingdom of God" (v. 5). To be "born again" is the same thing as being "born of water and the Spirit." The parallelism is deliberate, and the phrase "born of water and the Spirit" is simply Jesus' explanation of the *second* birth. In order to understand the expression "water and the Spirit," we have to ask how Nicodemus would have understood it.

There are two famous passages in the Old Testament where the words *water* and *Spirit* are brought together in a way that makes sense of this passage. One is Isaiah 44:3, which uses a poetic parallelism to equate the two terms, by making water a symbol of the Holy Spirit: "I will pour water on him who is thirsty, and floods on the dry ground; I will pour My Spirit on your descendants." The Holy Spirit is frequently depicted in the Old Testament being poured out like water (cf. Proverbs 1:23; Joel 2:28–29; Zechariah 12:10). So to a Jewish teacher steeped in the language of the Old Testament, the idea of being "born of water and the Spirit" would evoke the idea of an outpouring of God's Spirit—which is precisely what Jesus was saying.

But the key Old Testament text on this—the one I'm convinced Jesus was alluding to, and the one that almost certainly came to Nicodemus's mind—was an important and familiar passage: Ezekiel 36:25–27. There the Lord is affirming the promise of the new covenant to Israel, and He says:

> I will sprinkle clean water on you, and you shall be clean; I will cleanse you from all your filthiness and from all your idols. I will give you a new heart and put a new spirit within you; I will take the heart of stone out of your flesh and give you a heart of flesh. I will put My Spirit within you and cause you to walk in My statutes, and you will keep My judgments and do them.

That passage speaks of regeneration, the spiritual awakening of a dead soul. And that is the very truth Jesus was pressing upon Nicodemus. He was confronting this leading Pharisee with the truth that he needed a whole new heart—new *life;* not just a cosmetic makeover or another ritual added to an already-oppressive system of pharisaical spiritual disciplines, but a wholesale spiritual renewal so vast and dramatic that it can only be described as a second birth. With Ezekiel 36 as context, Jesus' juxtaposition of *water* and *Spirit* makes perfect sense. He was intentionally pointing Nicodemus to the familiar truth of that key promise about the new covenant.

To borrow a precisely parallel New Testament expression, *water* and *Spirit* are best understood as a reference to "the washing of regeneration and renewing of the Holy Spirit" (Titus 3:5). In all likelihood, Nicodemus, thoroughly familiar with Ezekiel's prophecy, now understood exactly what Jesus was telling him.

Another Difficult Saying from Jesus

Jesus continued by further emphasizing that spiritual rebirth is wholly a work of God, not the result of human effort: "That which is born of the flesh is flesh, and that which is born of the Spirit is spirit" (John 3:6). Jesus was merely stating a truth which, on reflection, ought to be self-evident. Flesh begets flesh. Living beings all reproduce "each according to its kind" (Genesis 1:24). By the very nature of things, therefore, *spiritual life* cannot be the fruit of human achievement, a fact that contradicts every form of works-religion, including the fundamental belief system of the Pharisees.

On top of that, Jesus added, because spiritual rebirth is a work of the Spirit, it is beyond the control of either human works or human willpower: "The wind blows where it wishes, and you hear the sound of it, but cannot tell where it comes from and where it goes. So is everyone who is born of the Spirit" (v. 8). The *effects* of the wind may be observed, but its boundaries cannot be discerned by human senses, and the wind itself can neither be harnessed nor directed by human efforts or ingenuity. The Holy Spirit's ministry operates in a similar fashion. He is sovereign and moves where He wishes, not at the whim of any human agenda. His workings are not contained in— or automatically dispensed through—any religious rituals or ceremonial protocols. In fact, the Spirit isn't moved by what *we* do at all, but by His own sovereign will.

To a typical Pharisee, what Jesus was saying to Nicodemus would likely have come across as highly offensive. Jesus was attacking the very core of Nicodemus's belief system, plainly implying that Nicodemus was lost, spiritually lifeless, and ultimately no better off in his rigid Pharisaism than an utterly immoral Gentile without God. (Indeed, Jesus made that very point quite often in his dealings with the religious leaders.)

This was a direct answer to Nicodemus's questions ("How can a man be born when he is old? Can he enter a second time into his mother's womb and be born?"). Jesus was telling Nicodemus, in language Nicodemus was sure to grasp, that not only was He not speaking of any superficial or fleshly self-reformation, but He was in fact calling for something Nicodemus was powerless to do *for himself.* This punctured the heart of Nicodemus's religious convictions. To a Pharisee like him, the worst imaginable news would be that there was nothing he could possibly do to help himself spiritually.

Jesus had basically equated this distinguished Pharisee with the most debased and dissipated kind of sinner. He had described Nicodemus's case as utterly hopeless. Talk about harsh!

But that is, after all, the very starting point of the gospel message. Sinners are "dead in trespasses and sins . . . by nature children of wrath . . . having no hope and without God" (Ephesians 2:1, 3, 12). This is one of the universal effects of Adam's sin on his offspring (Romans 5:12). We are born with sinful tendencies and fallen hearts, and we all sin. "All have sinned and fall short of the glory of God" (Romans 3:23). "There is none righteous, no, not one" (v. 10). "All we like sheep have gone astray" (Isaiah 53:6).

Furthermore, Scripture says we are hopeless to redeem ourselves, atone for our own sin, reform our hearts and minds, or earn any kind of merit in the eyes of God. Romans 8:7–8 says, "The carnal mind is enmity against God; for it is not subject to the law of God, *nor indeed can be.* So then, those who are in the flesh *cannot please God."*

Let's face it: the idea that the entire human race is fallen and condemned is too harsh for most people's tastes. They would rather believe that people are fundamentally good. But Scripture says otherwise. We are hopelessly corrupted by sin. All who do not have Christ as Lord and Savior are in bondage to evil, condemned by a just God, and bound for hell. Jesus not only strongly implied those very things in His opening words to Nicodemus; before He had finished fully explaining the gospel that evening, He made His meaning explicit: "He who does not believe is condemned already" (John 3:18).

The Gospel Distilled for Nicodemus

Nicodemus's response was utter astonishment: "How can these things be?" (v. 9). It was not that he didn't understand what Jesus was saying. I think he got the message plainly enough. But it overthrew his deepest convictions and left him virtually speechless. That question ("How can these things be?") is the last thing we hear from Nicodemus in the narrative of John 3. He had nothing further to say.

No wonder. Jesus was about to deliver His most direct, personal, scolding barb at Nicodemus yet: "Are you the teacher of Israel, and do not know these things?" (v. 10). Everything Jesus had said to Nicodemus so far had a clear basis in the Old Testament. Nicodemus was one of the top biblical scholars in the nation. *How could he not know these things?* It sounds like a put-down. The average Pharisee would have taken it that way and lashed back at Jesus with insults, accusations, or otherwise contemptuous retorts.

Not Nicodemus. He was completely silenced by the rebuke. In fact, he more or less fades into the background of John's narrative. He is not mentioned again until chapter 7, where he appears in a meeting of the Sanhedrin, says a word in defense of Jesus, and is promptly shouted down (John 7:44–53).

Starting in John 3:11, Jesus gives Nicodemus a discourse on the gospel. John 3:16, of course, is famous for its stress on the love of God and the giving of Christ so that "whoever believes in Him should not perish but have everlasting life." That is the central truth of the gospel message and the promise that makes it good news. But it is *not* good news for those who remain in unbelief.

And Jesus clearly regarded Nicodemus as an unbeliever. "You do not believe," he said in verse 12, and Nicodemus made no protest against that judgment. It seems clear that his conscience was affirming the truth of Jesus' assessment. So it would have hit the Pharisee in a very personal way when Jesus went on to say:

> He who believes in Him is not condemned; but he who does not believe is condemned already, because he has not believed in the name of the only begotten Son of God. And this is the condemnation, that the light has come into the world, and men loved darkness rather than light, because their deeds were evil. For everyone practicing evil hates the light and does not come to the light, lest his deeds should be

exposed. But he who does the truth comes to the light, that his deeds may be clearly seen, that they have been done in God.

(John 3:18–21)

Thus Jesus' conversation with Nicodemus ends on a harsh and sobering note about the severe condemnation that rests on all unbelievers and hypocrites.

The Rest of the Story

If this were the only place we encounter Nicodemus in all of Scripture, we might conclude that he left without saying any more and remained in unbelief all his life.

Scripture gives us two more glimpses of the man, however. It is clear that despite Jesus' severity and directness with him—or perhaps because of it—Nicodemus retained an interest in Jesus throughout the Lord's earthly ministry. And at some point he *did* believe, making the passage from death unto life. How and when this happened is not spelled out for us, but each of the biblical vignettes of Nicodemus shows him increasingly bold in separating himself from the rest of the Sanhedrin.

John 7 describes a meeting of the Sanhedrin in which the rest of the Pharisees were inveighing against Jesus and those who followed Him ("This crowd that does not know the law is accursed"—v. 49). They wanted Him arrested and brought before them, and it is clear that their one goal is to silence Him by whatever means they can. But one voice of dissent speaks on Jesus' behalf from within the Sanhedrin, and it is Nicodemus:

"Does our law judge a man before it hears him and knows what he is doing?" (v. 51).

For that, Nicodemus incurred the scorn of his fellow Pharisees, who shot back: "Are you also from Galilee? Search and look, for no prophet has arisen out of Galilee" (v. 52). Clearly, they were not willing to entertain even a hint of possibility that Jesus might be from God—even though His miracles clearly affirmed His authority; even though they could not refute one word of His teaching; and even though they had no legitimate charge with which to indict Him. But as Jesus Himself said, "everyone practicing evil hates the light and does not come to the light, lest his deeds should be exposed" (John 3:20).

There is every reason to conclude that Nicodemus, who originally came to Jesus under cover of darkness, was eventually drawn to the True Light and became a genuine believer. The last time we meet Nicodemus in Scripture is in John 19:39, where he and Joseph of Arimathea hastily prepared the Savior's body for burial. It was an act that could well have cost him everything, at the very moment when the rest of the Sanhedrin had whipped public fury against Jesus into a murderous rage. He clearly had become a different man than he was when he first approached Jesus as an unbelieving Pharisee.

In the long term, then, Jesus' apparent harshness with Nicodemus was fully vindicated. Blunt, unvarnished directness was precisely what Nicodemus needed. No one else in all of Israel would dare speak that way to a religious leader of Nicodemus's stature. But Jesus was telling him the most important thing he could possibly hear, in a voice that rang with authority.

All the Pharisees and religious leaders in Israel needed a similar wake-up call, and that explains the tone of Jesus' dealings with them throughout the gospel accounts. Yet aside from Nicodemus, the gospels contain no other accounts of conversion among the Pharisees during Jesus' earthly ministry. Remember that Nicodemus came to Jesus near the start of our Lord's public ministry. Sadly, however, apart from this one conversation with Nicodemus, *all* Jesus' public interactions with the Pharisees ended badly, with the Pharisees being offended or angry. From this point on, every Pharisee and religious figure Jesus will deal with responds with hostility, outrage, indignation, and in the end, the ultimate act of violence.

Might Jesus have gained a more positive response from the Pharisees if He had shown them the kind of deference they demanded? What if He had sought common ground with them and focused only on what He could affirm in their belief system? There was, after all, a lot to affirm; the Pharisees weren't flirting with gross paganism like the Baal worshipers in Elijah's time. What if Jesus had stressed where they were *right* rather than constantly attacking what was *wrong* in their teaching? Is it possible that the Sanhedrin would have been more open to Jesus if He had not constantly used them as the epitome of all that was wrong with Israel spiritually?

But truth doesn't defeat error by waging a public relations campaign. The struggle between truth and error is *spiritual warfare,* and truth has no way to defeat falsehood except by exposing and refuting error and deceit. That calls for candor and clarity, boldness and precision—and sometimes more severity than congeniality.

The fact that Nicodemus was the only Pharisee to listen

to Christ without being so offended that he turned completely against Him is no indictment of the way Jesus dealt with Israel's chief religious leaders. Rather, it is a gauge of how truly evil their whole system was. From here on, that becomes one of the central themes of all four gospel accounts.

God chooses not milksops destitute of backbone, to wear his glory upon their faces. We have plenty of men made of sugar, nowadays, that melt into the stream of popular opinion; but these shall never ascend into the hill of the Lord, nor stand in his holy place, nor wear the tokens of his glory.

—Charles H. Spurgeon

Four

THIS MAN SPEAKS BLASPHEMIES

Now it happened on a certain day, as He was teaching,
that there were Pharisees and teachers of the law sitting
by, who had come out of every town of Galilee, Judea,
and Jerusalem.
LUKE 5:17

Most of our Lord's early ministry took place in Galilee, where
(at first) He was out from under the constant scrutiny of the
Jerusalem-based Sanhedrin. The Gospels are sparse in the
details they record about those months. This is when Jesus
gathered most of His closest disciples (Matthew 4:18–22; Mark
1:16–20). Three Gospels record that He cast out demons, did
countless miracles, and ministered constantly to large crowds
during that first year (Matthew 4:23–24; Mark 1:39–45; Luke
5:15). Beyond that, the biblical record gives only a few specifics.

But as Jesus gained fame and followers, the religious leaders at some early point seem to have taken measures to keep
Him under surveillance wherever He went. All of a sudden,
every time He appeared in public—even in the remotest corners of Galilee—Pharisees were always present. His conflicts

with scribes and Pharisees soon began to increase steadily in both frequency and intensity.

A key thing to notice is that so far, the scribes and Pharisees have done nothing overt to provoke any conflict with Jesus. *He* incited that first clash with them in Jerusalem by driving the money changers from the temple without a single word of warning or prior announcement. The only personal interaction recorded between Jesus and an individual Pharisee was the dialogue with Nicodemus, who came on friendly terms—and Jesus rebuked him. For many months, that pattern continued. Every open conflict Jesus had with the Pharisees was instigated by Him, including the first major Galilean conflict between Jesus and the Jewish leaders—in which case He publicly embarrassed some Pharisees based on His knowledge of what they were *thinking*. Matthew, Mark, and Luke all describe the incident, but Luke's account is the fullest.

Luke has a lot to say about the Pharisees and their opposition to Christ, but chapter 5 in his Gospel is where he first introduces them. The setting is sometime after Jesus has returned to Galilee following that first Passover in Jerusalem. We can't tell precisely how much time has elapsed, but a careful harmony of the Gospels suggests that nearly a year and a half passed after that first temple assault before Jesus encountered overtly hostile Pharisees in Galilee.

Jesus' Move to Capernaum

Jesus had remained in Jerusalem for an unspecified time teaching, healing, and gathering disciples after the Passover feast.

Sometime in that interval after Passover is when the meeting with Nicodemus occurred.

Jesus then returned to Galilee via Samaria (John 4:3–4), taking a route no Pharisee would have taken. The Samaritans were considered unclean, and merely traveling through their land was thought by the Pharisees to be spiritually defiling. That was, of course, just one of many pharisaical taboos Jesus would break. But while traveling through Samaria, He had his famous encounter with the woman at the well in Sychar. That account consumes most of John 4. Christ led her to salvation— and she subsequently brought many in Sychar to Christ. Many of the villagers came to saving faith (John 4:39–42).

After two days' ministry in Sychar, Jesus finally returned to Galilee (v. 43). His childhood village, Nazareth, was a small, rural town, so He would have been well known to virtually everyone in the synagogue there, having grown up in their midst and attended that very synagogue every week of His young life. Luke expressly says it was His custom to go there on the Sabbath (4:16). Coming back now as a rabbi who was gaining renown and already accumulating many followers from all over Galilee, He no doubt piqued their curiosity by His mere presence.

But on that very first Sabbath back in His hometown, He caused a furor. He told the people,

> "You will surely say this proverb to Me, 'Physician, heal yourself! Whatever we have heard done in Capernaum, do also here in Your country.'" Then He said, "Assuredly, I say to you, no prophet is accepted in his own country. But I tell you truly, many widows

were in Israel in the days of Elijah, when the heaven was shut up three years and six months, and there was a great famine throughout all the land; but to none of them was Elijah sent except to Zarephath, in the region of Sidon, to a woman who was a widow. And many lepers were in Israel in the time of Elisha the prophet, and none of them was cleansed except Naaman the Syrian."

(vv. 23–27)

Notice: He portrayed Himself as a prophet comparable to Elijah—a Messenger from God not even accepted by His own people. He cast the people in the role of unbelievers—like the disobedient Israelites in Elijah's day who had bowed the knee to Baal. He spoke of God's sovereignty in bypassing all of Israel to minister to a single Gentile outcast, and strongly implied that they were in the same boat as the reprobate Israelites who were bypassed by Elijah's ministry.

The point He was making was not lost on the people of Nazareth. He was putting them in the same category as Baal-worshiping apostates.

The whole mood in Nazareth changed instantly: "All those in the synagogue, when they heard these things, were filled with wrath" (Luke 4:28). They drove Him out of the synagogue, to the outskirts of the city, and to the very edge of a cliff or rock ledge, where they intended to throw Him off. This was the first recorded major attempt on His life, and it came from the very community where He had grown up!

But just before they reached the edge of the rock precipice, Jesus miraculously eluded the mob. Simply "passing through the midst of them, He went His way" (v. 30). They were evidently confounded—temporarily blinded or supernaturally put into a state of confusion—and Jesus walked away from them without a struggle and with no pursuers.

In fact, He walked away from Nazareth completely. In the next verse, Luke says, "Then He went down to Capernaum, a city of Galilee, and was teaching them on the Sabbaths" (v. 31). In other words, He established His home base in Capernaum, on the north shore of the Sea of Galilee, some thirty miles from Nazareth. Matthew 4:13 says, "Leaving Nazareth, He came and *settled* in Capernaum" (NASB). After this, when we read a reference to "His own city" (Matthew 9:1), it's talking about Capernaum. Mark 2:1 says when Jesus was in Capernaum, He was "at home" (NASB).

Most of Jesus' closest disciples also called Capernaum home. It was where Zebedee, father of James and John, had his fishing business. It was where Peter and Andrew hailed from. It was if anything an even more insignificant and obscure village than Nazareth, but it was perfectly situated for One who delights to use "the foolish things of the world to put to shame the wise, . . . the weak things of the world to put to shame the things which are mighty; and the base things of the world and the things which are despised . . . [so] that no flesh should glory in His presence" (1 Corinthians 1:27–29).

Soon people flocked to Capernaum to see and hear Jesus. The crowds were so vast and so crushing on the shores of Galilee that the only way Jesus could preach to them without being utterly surrounded and swallowed up by a sea of humanity was to sit in a boat and do His teaching from just offshore. He cleansed lepers, healed all kinds of diseases, and taught the ever-increasing multitudes. Since there was never an infirmity He could not heal or a possessed person He could not deliver, the crowds continued to grow and pursue Him more aggressively than ever. "So He Himself often withdrew into the wilderness and prayed" (Luke 5:16).

What Luke describes is a tireless, nonstop campaign of daily teaching and public ministry. Naturally, news of Jesus' Galilean ministry reached all the way to Jerusalem and came to the attention of the Sanhedrin.

Enter the Pharisees

When Luke first mentions the "Pharisees and teachers of the law," they are watching Jesus from the sidelines. They have come to Capernaum, not as part of the normal crowd seeking to benefit from Jesus' ministry, but as critical observers, looking for reasons to condemn Him, and if possible thwart Him, before He became any more popular. It is clear that they had formed this agenda ahead of time, because they coordinated their arrival "on a certain day . . . out of every town of Galilee, Judea, and Jerusalem" (Luke 5:17).

Jesus was in Capernaum, in a house. Mark seems to suggest that it was the house where Jesus Himself lived (Mark 2:1). As usual, the press of the crowds was suffocating, and Jesus was preaching from within the house to as many people as could gather within earshot. Mark describes the scene: "Many were gathered together, so that there was no longer space, not even near the door; and He was speaking the word to them" (v. 2 NASB). Luke adds, "And the power of the Lord was present to heal them" (Luke 5:17).

Here's a pattern you will notice in almost every confrontation between Jesus and Pharisees: in one way or another, His deity is always at the heart of the conflict. It is as if He deliberately provokes them with claims, statements, or actions that He knows they will object to, and then He uses the resulting conflict to demonstrate that all the authority He claimed did indeed belong to Him.

On this occasion, the issue at stake was the forgiveness of sins. Remember that Jesus had been performing public healings for several weeks all over Galilee. There was no question about His ability to heal any disease or deliver the spiritually downtrodden from any kind of demonic bondage. Demons and disease alike always fled at His Word—sometimes even at His presence. "Wherever He entered, into villages, cities, or the country, they laid the sick in the marketplaces, and begged Him that they might just touch the hem of His garment. And as many as touched Him were made well" (Mark 6:56). In Jesus' own words, this was the proof of all His claims and the confirmation of all His teaching: "The blind see, the lame walk, the lepers are cleansed, the deaf hear, the dead are raised, the poor have the gospel preached to them" (Luke 7:22).

On this particular day, however, Jesus was presented with a particularly difficult case—a tragic and incurable affliction so debilitating that the sick man had to be carried on a stretcher by four other men. The crowd was so concentrated and so tightly drawn to Jesus in order to hear, it would have been well nigh impossible for one healthy man to squeeze through and get next to Jesus, much less four men carrying a quadriplegic on a stretcher.

It may well be that forgiveness was the very topic Jesus was teaching about. The subject was certainly in the air. Immediately before this, after teaching from Peter's boat, Jesus had instructed Peter to launch out into the deep and let down his nets (Luke 5:4). To any fisherman such a strategy would sound foolish. Fish were best netted at night, in shallow waters, while they were feeding. Peter had fished all night and caught nothing. During daylight hours, the fish would migrate to much deeper, cooler waters, where it would normally be impossible to reach them with nets. "Nevertheless," Peter said, "at Your word I will let down the net" (v. 5). When the haul of fishes was so great that the nets began to break, Peter was instantly smitten with the realization that he was in the presence of divine power—and the first thing he was aware of was the weight of his own guilt. "He fell down at Jesus' knees, saying, "Depart from me, for I am a sinful man, O Lord!" (v. 8).

Forgiveness was also one of Jesus' favorite subjects to preach about. It was one of the key themes in His Sermon on the Mount. It was a focus of the Lord's Prayer and the subject He expounded on at the end of that prayer (Matthew 6:14–15). It's the central theme that dominates all of Luke 5. If forgiveness was not the very subject Jesus was preaching on, it was nevertheless about to become the topic of the day.

Now imagine the Pharisees, sitting somewhere on the periphery, watching and listening for things to criticize as these four men carrying the stretcher arrived on the scene.

Who Can Forgive Sins But God?

If they wanted to see Jesus in action, these Pharisees had certainly come on the right day. Here was a hopelessly paralyzed man who had been brought from some distance by four other men whose journey from another village could not have been an easy one. And when they arrived, they must have seen instantly that they had no hope of getting close to Jesus by any conventional method. Even if they waited until Jesus left the house, the crowds were much too thick and too electrified to make way for five men to penetrate all the way to the center of the vast throng that surrounded Jesus wherever He went.

The fact that the man was carried on a pallet rather than seated in some kind of cart suggests that he was probably a quadriplegic, totally paralyzed in all his limbs—perhaps as a result of some injury to his neck. He was a classic object lesson about the fallen human condition. He was unable to move, utterly reliant on the grace and goodness of others, completely impotent to do anything whatsoever for himself.

Furthermore, the man's muscles would be atrophied and shriveled to nothing from nonuse. If Jesus could heal him, it would be instantly obvious to all that a true miracle had taken place.

The sheer desperation of the man and his four friends can be measured by what they did when they realized they would not be able to get close to Jesus. They went up to the roof. In order for four men to ascend with a stretcher, there must have been an external stairway leading to a veranda or walkway. Even at that, it would be a difficult ascent. But this was evidently a substantial house, with a typical Mediterranean-style upper-level patio adjacent to a tiled section of roof. That afforded the men exactly the opportunity they needed. They carried the man upstairs, determined approximately where Jesus was below them, and began removing the tiles over that part of the roof.

What a dramatic entrance this was! It no doubt startled the crowd when the roof began to open up. The gap in the roof needed to be large enough for the man and his stretcher—which likely meant that not only the external roof tiles but also some of the underlying lattice-work supporting the tiles had to be carefully removed. A tile roof was no cheap or temporary covering, and there's simply no way to open a hole in a tile roof like that without lots of debris and dust falling into the crowd below. We would normally expect both the crowd and the landlord to be annoyed by the actions of these men.

But in Jesus' eyes, this was clear evidence of great faith. All three Synoptic Gospels record this incident, and all three say Jesus *"saw* their faith" (Luke 5:20; Matthew 9:2; Mark 2:5). He saw faith reflected in their persistence and determination, of course. After all the work they had done to lay their friend at Jesus' feet, it was obvious to everyone what they were there for: they had brought the man for physical healing. Anyone who thought about it could see it required some degree of faith in Jesus' healing ability to go to all that work.

But the text is suggesting that Jesus saw something even deeper. Because He is God incarnate, He could also see into their hearts, perceive their motives, and even know their thoughts—just as He had seen into the heart of Nicodemus.

What He saw as these men lowered their friend from the ceiling was true faith—repentant faith. Not one of the gospel accounts suggests that either the paralyzed man or his friends said a word. There was no verbal testimony from the man about his repentance. There was no statement of contrition. There was no confession of sin. There was no affirmation of faith in God. There was no verbal cry for mercy. There didn't need to be; Jesus could see into the man's heart and mind. He knew that the Holy Spirit had done a work in the paralyzed man's heart. The man had come to Jesus with a broken and contrite spirit. He wanted to be right with God. He did not even need to say that. Jesus knew it because as God, He knows all hearts.

Here was an opportunity for Jesus to display His deity. Everyone could see the man's *affliction;* only Jesus could see his *faith.* Without any comment either from the paralytic man at Jesus' feet or from the four men peering through the hole in the roof, Jesus turned to the paralytic man and said, "Man, your sins are forgiven you" (Luke 5:20).

He freely forgave him. He fully justified him. With those words, the man's sins were obliterated from his account, wiped off the divine books. On His own personal authority, Jesus instantly absolved that man of all the guilt of all his sins forever.

With that claim, Jesus gave the scribes and Pharisees exactly what they were waiting for: an opportunity to accuse Him. And make no mistake: Jesus' words to the paralytic would be deeply shocking to the Pharisees' religion by any measure. In the first place, if He were not God incarnate, it would indeed be the very height of blasphemy for Him to pretend He had authority to forgive sins. In the second place, the Pharisees' religion was strongly oriented toward works—so that in their view, forgiveness must be *earned.* It was unthinkable to them

that forgiveness could ever be granted immediately and unconditionally by faith alone.

According to Matthew, some of the scribes who were there
reacted "at once" (9:3). But curiously, in this instance, they did
not rise up and shout out a verbal protest. It was still early in
Jesus' ministry, and they constituted a small enough minority
on the fringe of this crowd in Jesus' own community that their
initial reaction seems surprisingly subdued. If their shock registered at all, it was only on their faces. Luke says they "began to
reason, saying, 'Who is this who speaks blasphemies? Who can
forgive sins but God alone?'" (5:21). Matthew makes it clear
that they said these things "within themselves"—not aloud
(9:3). Mark likewise says, "The scribes were sitting there and
reasoning in their hearts, 'Why does this Man speak blasphemies like this? Who can forgive sins but God alone?'" (Mark
2:6–7). In their minds collectively they were all thinking the
same thing. *This is blasphemy of the worst kind. Who but God
can legitimately forgive sins?*

The question was merely rhetorical; they weren't really
wondering what the answer might be. They knew full well
that no one can forgive sins except God. Their doctrine on that
point was sound enough. You and I can individually forgive
whatever wrongs are done to us as far as our own personal
claims for justice are concerned, but we don't have the authority
to absolve anyone from guilt before the throne of God. No man
can do that. No priest can do that. No one can do that but God
alone. Anyone who claims that prerogative is either God or a
blasphemer. In fact, for someone who is not God, this would
indeed be the supreme act of blasphemous idolatry—putting
himself in the place of God.

Who Is This?

Jesus had deliberately put Himself at the center of a scenario that would force every observer to render a verdict about Him. That's true not only of the people who were eyewitnesses in Capernaum that day but also for those who simply read this account in Scripture. And the choice is clear. There are only two possible conclusions we can make with regard to Christ: He is either God incarnate, or He is a blasphemer and a fraud. There is no middle ground, and that is precisely the situation Jesus was aiming for.

There are a lot of people even today who want to patronize Jesus by saying He was a good person, an outstanding religious leader, an important prophet, a profound ethicist, a paragon of integrity, kindness, and decency—a *great* man, but still merely a man—not God incarnate. But this one episode in His public ministry is sufficient to erase that choice from the list of possibilities. He is either God or the ultimate blasphemer. He purposely erased every conceivable middle-way alternative.

Jesus did not scold the Pharisees for thinking that only God can forgive sin. They weren't wrong about that. Nor did He write their concern off as a misunderstanding of His intention. Instead, He rebuked them for "think[ing] evil" about Him (Matthew 9:4). They were wrong to assume the worst about Him when in fact He had already often displayed the power of God convincingly and publicly by healing diseases that no one but God could heal and by casting out demons that only God has power over. Instead of thinking, *No mere man can forgive sin. He just blasphemed,* they ought to have been asking themselves, *Can it possibly be that this is no mere man?*

55

All three Synoptics stress that Jesus read their thoughts (Matthew 9:4; Mark 2:8; Luke 5:22). Just as He knew the heart of the paralytic and understood that the man's first concern was for the salvation of his soul, He knew the hearts of the Pharisees and understood that their only motive was to find a way to accuse Him. The fact that He knew what they were thinking ought to have been another clue to them that He was no mere man.

But they were already thinking well past that. As far as they were concerned, this was a case of blasphemy pure and simple, and no other option even seems to have occurred to them. Moreover, if they could make *that* accusation stick, they could call for Him to be stoned. Open blasphemy was a capital crime. Leviticus 24:16 was emphatic about that: "Whoever blasphemes the name of the LORD shall surely be put to death."

Which Is Easier?

Before the scribes and Pharisees could even give voice to what they were thinking, Jesus Himself pressed the issue. "He answered and said to them, 'Why are you reasoning in your hearts? Which is easier, to say, "Your sins are forgiven you," or to say, "Rise up and walk"?'" (Luke 5:22–23).

They were thinking, *This man is blaspheming because He claims to do what only God can do.* Notice that Jesus did not even hint that they might have misunderstood His intentions. He did not double back and try to qualify His own statement. Nor did He challenge their belief that only God can forgive sin. As a matter of fact, they were exactly right about that.

Of course, only God can infallibly read human hearts, too. In Ezekiel 11:5, God Himself says, "I know the things that come into your mind." He speaks again in Jeremiah 17:10: "I, the LORD, search the heart, I test the mind." No human has the ability to see perfectly into the mind of another like that. "The LORD does not see as man sees; for man looks at the outward appearance, but the LORD looks at the heart" (1 Samuel 16:7). Jesus had just displayed knowledge both of the paralytic's mind and their own secret thoughts about Him. Shouldn't that have made them pause and reflect on who this was that they were dealing with?

That is precisely what Jesus was challenging them to consider. He proposed a simple test: "Which is easier, to say, 'Your sins are forgiven you,' or to say, 'Rise up and walk'?" (Luke 5:23). While it is certainly true that only God can forgive sins, it is likewise true that only God can perform the kind of regenerative miracle necessary to restore the atrophied muscles and brittle bones of a quadriplegic to perfect wholeness in a split second—so that he could literally rise up and walk on command. The question was not whether Jesus could make this man *better,* but whether He could instantly make him whole and healthy.

Even with the best methods of modern medicine, if someone happens to recover the ability to move after suffering a catastrophic injury of the sort that causes severe paralysis, it usually takes months of therapy for the brain to rediscover how to send accurate signals through the injured nerve paths to the disabled limbs. Regardless of how long this man had been paralyzed, we might expect at the very least that he would need some time to learn how to walk again. But Jesus' healings always bypassed all such therapy. People born blind were given not only their sight but also the instant ability to make sense of what they saw (John 9:1–38; Mark 8:24–25). When Jesus healed a deaf person, He also immediately healed the resultant speech impediment—no therapy required (Mark 7:32–35). Whenever He healed lame people, He gave them not only regenerated muscle tissue, but also full strength and dexterity to walk (Matthew 9:6–7; Mark 2:12). Even a man infirm and bedridden for thirty-eight years could simply pick up his pallet and walk away (John 5:6–9).

That is just what this man needed: an act of divine, creative power such as only God can perform.

Notice carefully the way Jesus framed His question: "Which is easier to *say?*" He was picking at their thought process. They were indignant because He had granted this man forgiveness. They had never challenged His ability to heal. Obviously, no mere man has the power either to heal at will or to absolve sin at will. Healing a true paralytic is actually a perfect metaphor for forgiveness in that regard: humanly impossible. But Jesus could do either or both with equal authority.

Still, which is easier to *say?* Obviously, it's easier to tell someone his sins are forgiven, because no one can see if it actually happened.

The fact that Jesus knew their hearts so perfectly and yet refused to avert the public conflict they sought is significant. He knew full well that the Pharisees would be offended if He declared this man's sins forgiven, and yet He was not deterred from doing it. In fact, He did it as publicly as possible. He surely *could* have healed this man's infirmity without provoking that kind of open conflict with the Pharisees. He could have also dealt privately with the issue of the man's guilt, rather than making such a pronouncement within earshot of everyone. Jesus was surely aware that many people in a crowd that size would not be able to understand what He was doing or why He did it. At the very least, He could have taken time to pause and explain why He had a right to exercise divine authority. Any or all of those things would have at least avoided the perception that He was deliberately inflaming the Pharisees.

This kind of friction between Jesus and the religious elite of Israel could not possibly be edifying to the common fishermen and housewives of Capernaum, could it? A wise person would do everything in his power to avoid offending these Pharisees—right? What possible good could come from turning this man's deliverance into a theater of public controversy?

But Jesus had no such scruples. The point He was making was vastly more important than how the Pharisees or the people of Capernaum felt about it. Therefore, "'[So] that you may know that the Son of Man has power on earth to forgive sins'—He said to the man who was paralyzed, 'I say to you, arise, take up your bed, and go to your house'" (Luke 5:24).

Now, it is not at all easy to say to someone like this, "Arise, take up your bed, and go." Because if you say that and he doesn't do it straightaway, you have just revealed that you have no authority to do what you are claiming. But if Jesus could heal this man, He would thereby demonstrate in the most graphic and public way possible that He has authority to do what only God can do.

The Critics Silenced

Luke's account is notable for its straightforward simplicity. The writing style mirrors the startling suddenness of the miracle. Everything from this point on in the narrative happens so quickly that Luke covers it all in two short verses. Of the paralytic, Luke says, *"Immediately* he rose up before them, took up what he had been lying on, and departed to his own house, glorifying God" (5:25).

A lot happened in that one instant. The man's bones, fragile from nonuse, hardened perfectly. His muscles were restored at once to full strength and functionality. His joints and tendons became sturdy and mobile. All the elements of his physiology that had atrophied were regenerated. His nervous system switched back on and immediately became fully functional. Neuron fibers that had long ago ceased to feel anything sprang instantly back to life. One moment he felt nothing in those useless extremities; the next moment he felt all the strength and energy that comes with perfect health. Arms that one minute before had needed to be borne by four men and a stretcher suddenly were able to carry the stretcher back home.

The man's departure seems awfully abrupt. But Jesus' command consisted of three simple imperatives: "Arise, take up your bed, and go to your house" (v. 24). And that is precisely what the man did. If he paused to thank Jesus, he did not stop for long. We know for a fact that he was deeply grateful. But he was also understandably eager to get home and show his loved ones what God had done for Him.

Luke doesn't say how far away his home was, but it must have been a wonderful walk. And here's where we see his profound gratitude: all the way home he was "glorifying God" (v. 25).

The Bible sometimes understates the obvious things: "glorifying God." That's what the angels did in heaven when they announced the birth of the Messiah (Luke 2:13–14). It's easy to envision this man running, leaping, clapping, and dancing all the way home. If his four friends went home with him, he probably outran them all. They must have been a little fatigued from carrying him to Capernaum; he was newly reborn, freshly invigorated, and relieved of every burden he had ever borne except that now-useless stretcher.

"Glorifying God" would also have involved lots of noise— laughing, shouting, and singing hallelujahs. I imagine he could hardly wait to run to his front door, throw it open with a shout of gladness, burst in with his new arms held wide, and celebrate his new wholeness with his wife, his kids, or whatever family he had at home.

But the *best* part was not that he could skip home; the best part was that he was cleansed of his sin. I don't know what all he had dared to hope for when he and the four erstwhile pall-bearers started out that morning. But I'm fairly certain he did not expect what he got. All his sins were forgiven and he had been created new. No wonder he glorified God.

The miracle had a corresponding effect on the people of Capernaum. "They were all amazed, and they glorified God and were filled with fear, saying, 'We have seen strange things today!'" (v. 26). The Greek expression Luke used means "seized with astonishment." The noun in that phrase is *ekstasis,* which of course is the root of the English word *ecstasy.* It literally speaks of a mind jolt—a powerful shock of amazement and profound delight. In this case, however, to translate the word as *ecstatic* would not really capture the people's reaction as Luke pictures it. It was more like stunned shock—mixed with fear and wonder.

Like the formerly paralyzed man, they glorified God. The praise of the crowd, however, is of a different character from the healed man's worship. He was moved by deep personal gratitude and a heart freshly delivered from guilt. They were simply in awe of the strangeness of what they had seen. We know from subsequent events that most of Capernaum's admiration for Jesus would turn out to be a fickle sort of esteem. Many in that crowd were halfhearted disciples and hangers-on who would quickly fall away when Jesus' teaching became harder.

But most peculiar is the fact that Luke says nothing more about the Pharisees. With a kind of stealth that will soon become a pattern, they simply lapse into utter silence and fade out of the story. The man who was healed went home one way, glorifying God and rejoicing in his newfound robe of righteousness. The religious leaders of Israel slunk away in the opposite direction— silently seething with anger, resentful that Jesus had pronounced the paralytic forgiven, unable even to rejoice in the man's good fortune, and silently plotting their next attempt to discredit Jesus. We know that was their response, because when they show up again, they will be a little more angry, a lot more exercised, and a lot less open to any serious consideration of Jesus' claims. This first Galilean controversy seems to mark the start of a pattern of increasingly hostile public conflicts with Jesus whereby their hearts would be completely hardened against Him.

This occasion also fairly summed up the spiritual reasons for the Pharisees' intense hatred of Jesus. They could not stand the compassion that would forgive a sinner on the spot. The idea that Jesus would instantly and freely justify a paralytic—someone who by definition was unable to work—contradicted everything they stood for. Jesus' exercise of divine authority also rankled them. It was not so much that they really believed Him guilty of blasphemy—after all, He answered that charge by repeatedly and convincingly proving He had full power to do what only God can do. But they had their own idea of what God should be like, and Jesus simply didn't fit the profile. Besides all that, He was a threat to their status in Israel (John 11:48)—and the more He humiliated them in public this way, the more their own influence diminished. From here on, that reality loomed as an urgent crisis in all their thoughts about Him.

After this episode, critical Pharisees become commonplace in all the gospel narratives. They soon began to dog Jesus' steps everywhere He went, seizing every reason they could find to accuse Him, opposing Him at every turn, even resorting to lies and blasphemy in their desperation to discredit Him.

Clearly, they had already written Him off completely. If they would not acknowledge Him when they saw a dramatic miracle like the instant healing of this paralytic, nothing would penetrate their hardened, self-righteous hearts. They were already well down the path that would make them the chief conspirators in His murder.

Jesus, of course, embodied *all* the attributes of God—kindness, longsuffering, and mercy on the one hand; wrath, righteousness, and judgment on the other. All those qualities are discernible in some measure in the way He dealt with the Pharisees over the course of His ministry. But because the

63

gospel was at stake and His own lordship was constantly under attack from these men who were the most influential spiritual leaders in the nation, His tenderness never overshadowed His severity in any of His dealings with them.

Their course was fixed, apparently sometime before this first Galilean encounter with Him. Their hearts were already set to be unyielding to His authority, oblivious to His teaching, opposed to His truth, insensitive to His righteousness, and impervious to His rebukes. They had essentially written Him off already.

He would soon write them off as well.

Brethren, the Savior's character has all goodness in all perfection; he is full of grace and truth. Some men, nowadays, talk of him as if he were simply incarnate benevolence. It is not so. No lips ever spoke with such thundering indignation against sin as the lips of the Messiah. "He is like a refiner's fire, and like fuller's soap. His fan is in his hand, and he will thoroughly purge his floor." While in tenderness he prays for his tempted disciple, that his faith may not fail, yet with awful sternness he winnows the heap, and drives away the chaff into unquenchable fire. We speak of Christ as being meek and lowly in spirit, and so he was. A bruised reed he did not break, and the smoking flax he did not quench; but his meekness was balanced by his courage, and by the boldness with which he denounced hypocrisy. "Woe unto you, Scribes and Pharisees, hypocrites; ye fools and blind, ye serpents, ye generation of vipers, how can ye escape the damnation of hell?" These are not the words of the

*milksop some authors represent Christ to have been. He is
a man—a thorough man throughout—a God-like man—
gentle as a woman, but yet stern as a warrior in the midst
of the day of battle. The character is balanced; as much of
one virtue as of another. As in Deity every attribute is full
orbed; justice never eclipses mercy, nor mercy justice, nor
justice faithfulness; so in the character of Christ you have
all the excellent things.*

—**Charles H. Spurgeon**

Five

BREAKING THE SABBATH

He not only broke the Sabbath, but also said that God was His Father, making Himself equal with God.
JOHN 5:18

Matthew, Mark, and Luke all record that the healing of the paralytic was followed immediately by the call and conversion of Matthew. Until Jesus called him to discipleship, Matthew would have been one of the most hated men in the entire Galilean region. He was a tax collector (a *publican,* to use the familiar terminology of the King James Version). He was therefore regarded by the entire community as a despicable traitor to the Jewish nation. He was the polar opposite of the Pharisees, in just about every conceivable way.

Mark refers to Matthew as "Levi the son of Alphaeus" (Mark 2:14). That, together with the fact that the gospel he wrote is thoroughly Jewish in style and content, indicates that Matthew was a Hebrew by birth. But he was a willing agent of Caesar, in league with Israel's oppressors in order to facilitate their evil occupation of the promised land and make money for himself at the expense of Israel's people.

Rome's system of taxation was utterly corrupt. Tariffs were ambiguously assessed and inconsistently levied through a method that seemed more like extortion than anything else. Tax collectors were overwhelmingly crooked, well known for using their office to line their own pockets. Officially, Rome looked the other way and allowed them to do that. After all, corruption greased the wheels of their aggressive revenue-producing machine. And Matthew was a big cog in the Galilean component of that apparatus.

Everything about Matthew would have been odious to faithful Israelites. As a matter of fact, publicans were the lowest and most despised of all the social outcasts in all the land. They were considered the most despicable of sinners, and they often lived up to that reputation in every conceivable sense. Pharisees and common people alike viewed them with the utmost scorn.

Not only do all three Synoptic Gospels place the call of Matthew immediately after the healing of the paralytic; both Matthew and Luke indicate that what follows happened immediately, on that same day. *"As Jesus passed on from there,* He saw a man named Matthew sitting at the tax office" (Matthew 9:9). *"After these things* He went out and saw a tax collector named Levi, sitting at the tax office" (Luke 5:27). Apparently, as soon as the paralyzed man picked up his pallet and left for home, Jesus went out of the house where the healing had taken place and started toward the lakeshore. In a village as small as Capernaum, situated right at water's edge, that could not be more than a few blocks. Mark indicates that Jesus' plan was to continue teaching the multitudes, and the waterfront obviously afforded a better, more suitable venue than a house for that. As "He went out again by the sea" (Mark 2:13), somewhere along the way "He saw Levi the son of Alphaeus sitting at the tax office" (v. 14).

Matthew was perhaps the least likely person in all of Capernaum to become one of Jesus' twelve closest followers. The other disciples, mostly fishermen from Capernaum, undoubtedly knew him well, and they must have despised the way he had made himself wealthy off their livelihood.

"Follow Me!"

But on that day, as Jesus passed the tax office, He caught Matthew's eye and gave him a simple two-word greeting: "Follow Me!" All three accounts of this incident record just that; no more. Matthew was obviously a man already under conviction. He had borne the weight of sin and guilt long enough, and upon hearing that simple command from Jesus, "he left all, rose up, and followed Him" (Luke 5:28).

For a man in Matthew's position, leaving everything behind so quickly was a dramatic turnaround comparable to the paralytic's sudden ability to walk and carry his own stretcher. Matthew's heart change was a *spiritual* rebirth, but no less miraculous than the paralytic's instant physical healing. As far as Matthew's career was concerned, this was a total and irreversible change of course. You could not walk away from a Roman tax commission and then have second thoughts and ask for your office back two days later. But Matthew did not hesitate. His sudden repentance is one of the most dramatic conversions described anywhere in Scripture.

In a village the size of Capernaum (fewer than two hundred yards from water's edge to the northern perimeter of the village), it is virtually certain that Matthew's office was very near the house where Jesus healed the paralytic. Given the commotion of the crowd, it would be impossible for the events of that day to escape Matthew's notice.

Matthew must have perked up when Jesus declared the paralytic man's sins forgiven. We can discern from his immediate response to Jesus that he was utterly fed up with the life of sin. He was probably feeling the spiritual barrenness that goes with ill-gotten material wealth. And it is clear that he was sensing the weight of his own guilt under the Holy Spirit's conviction. Jesus had just granted a forlorn quadriplegic the very thing Matthew's own soul craved: forgiveness, cleansing, and a pronouncement of justification. Coming from Someone like Jesus who obviously had the authority to back up His decrees, that would definitely have caught Matthew's attention. Clearly, before Jesus even walked by and spoke to him, Matthew was being drawn to faith because of what he had seen that day.

Matthew's perspective was the polar opposite of the Pharisees'. He yearned to be free from his sin. They would not even admit that they were sinners. No wonder Matthew's response to Jesus was so immediate.

Why Does He Consort with Publicans and Sinners?

Matthew decided to host a celebratory reception for Jesus that very day. Like all new converts, he desperately wanted to introduce as many of his friends as possible to Jesus without delay. So he opened his home and invited Jesus as guest of honor. Luke says "a great number of tax collectors and others" came to the banquet (Luke 5:29). The "others" would of course be the kind of lowlifes who were willing to socialize with a group of publicans. In other words, this gathering would not have included any of the regulars from the local synagogue.

That a rabbi would be willing to fraternize at a party with such people was utterly repugnant to the Pharisees. It was diametrically opposed to all their doctrines about separation and ceremonial uncleanness. Here was yet another pet issue of the Pharisees, and Jesus was openly violating their standards, knowing full well that they were watching Him closely. From their perspective, it must have seemed as if He were deliberately flaunting His contempt for their system.

Because He was. Remember: all the friction that has taken place out in the open thus far between Jesus and Israel's religious elite has been entirely at *His* instigation. As far as we know from Scripture, they had not yet voiced a single unprovoked criticism or public accusation against Him.

Even now, the Pharisees were not yet bold enough to complain to Jesus directly. They sought out His disciples and murmured their protest to them. It was a craven attempt to blindside Jesus by provoking a debate with His followers instead. I like the way Luke says it: "The Pharisees and their scribes began grumbling at His disciples" (Luke 5:30 NASB).

But Jesus overheard (Matthew 9:12; Mark 2:17), and He answered the Pharisees directly, with a single statement that became the definitive motto for His interaction with the self-righteous Sanhedrin and their ilk: "It is not those who are healthy who need a physician, but those who are sick; I did not come to call the righteous, but sinners" (Mark 2:17 NASB). For sinners and tax collectors seeking relief from the burden of their sin, Jesus had nothing but good news. To the self-righteous religious experts, He had nothing to say at all.

Harsh? Yes it was. There was virtually no possibility that a comment like this would help sway the Pharisees to Jesus' point of view. It was likelier to increase their hostility against Him.

And yet it was the *right* thing for Him to say at this moment. It was the truth they needed to hear. The fact that they were not "open" to it did not alter Jesus' commitment to speaking the truth without toning it down.

The Pharisees evidently had no answer for Jesus. None of the gospels record anything further that they said. Here again, they simply lapse into silence and fade into the background of the narrative.

Their strategy when embarrassed like this seemed to be that they would fall back, regroup, and simply look for a different way to accuse Him. Each time, they would come back more determined and a little more bold.

Their attempts to discredit Jesus were by no means over. In fact, the Pharisees had only *begun* to fight.

The Conflict Crystallizes

Sometime not long after that momentous day in Capernaum, Jesus made another journey into Judea. John is the only one of the gospel writers to mention that Jesus went to Jerusalem (again, to celebrate one of the annual feast days) near the midpoint of His three-year ministry. The incident is recorded in chapter 5 of John's gospel. Verse 1 says, "There was a feast of the Jews, and Jesus went up to Jerusalem." That visit to

Jerusalem resulted in Jesus' next major showdown with the Sanhedrin.

John frequently catalogues events in Jesus' life by the feast days. He mentions six of them, and this is the only one he does not identify by name. The phrase "a feast of the Jews" could be describing that year's Passover feast. More likely, this was the Feast of Tabernacles—the harvest festival. It becomes a crucial turning point in Jesus' conflict with the Sanhedrin. After this incident, they were not content merely to discredit Him; they were determined to put Him to death (John 5:18). From that point on, their challenges to His authority would be open, brazen, and increasingly shrill.

Likewise, the rebukes and admonitions Jesus aimed their way would become more and more severe from this point forward.

This incident, in some ways an echo of the previous one, started with the healing of a man who had been completely bedridden for thirty-eight years (v. 5). The miracle took place at the pool of Bethesda, near the Sheep Gate at the northeastern corner of the temple grounds. It was very close to the place where the sheep market was—where Jesus had driven out the money changers approximately eighteen months before. John writes,

> Now there is in Jerusalem by the Sheep Gate a pool, which is called in Hebrew, Bethesda, having five porches. In these lay a great multitude of sick people, blind, lame, paralyzed . . . . Now a certain man was there who had an infirmity thirty-eight years. When Jesus saw him lying there, and knew that he already

had been in that condition a long time, He said to him, "Do you want to be made well?"

The sick man answered Him, "Sir, I have no man to put me into the pool when the water is stirred up; but while I am coming, another steps down before me."

Jesus said to him, "Rise, take up your bed and walk." And immediately the man was made well, took up his bed, and walked.

(John 5:2–3, 5–9)

This is the only mention of Bethesda in Scripture. The existence of the pool—a large cistern surrounded by five covered colonnades—was questioned by skeptics until archaeologists discovered it in the nineteenth century, complete with the ruins of the five porticoes.

Verse 4 of that passage says, "An angel went down at a certain time into the pool and stirred up the water; then whoever stepped in first, after the stirring of the water, was made well of whatever disease he had." That verse is not in the earliest and most reliable New Testament manuscripts. It appears to be a scribe's marginal explanatory note that found its way into the body of the text in later copies. Nowhere else is there any mention of an angel or any supernatural healing effect from the waters.

Nevertheless, the pool was a magnet for the sick and infirm. It was fed by an intermittent spring of warm mineral water, and when the waters began to stir, it signified a fresh infusion of soothing warmth and minerals.

So the five porches sheltered "a great multitude of sick

people, blind, lame, paralyzed" (v. 3). Every one of them would undoubtedly have been glad to be healed. But on this occasion, Jesus bypassed them all and quietly singled out this one lone man.

The exact nature and extent of the man's disability is not given. He does not appear to have been completely paralyzed like the man in Capernaum. In verse 7 the man himself suggests that he had some ability to move, though only slowly and with great difficulty. He might have had a serious arthritic condition, a degenerative muscle disease, some kind of palsy, or a long-term disability from a major injury.

Whatever the precise nature of his affliction, it was severe enough to make it impossible for the man to move freely on his own. He was therefore essentially bedridden, and he had been like that for what seemed like a lifetime—thirty-eight years. Such a man would be unemployable and most likely poor. A spring-fed pool of warm mineral water was the cheapest, most effective therapy all the best medical expertise of that era could offer for a disability such as his. But there was a problem: whoever had brought him to Bethesda didn't stay with him, and thus he was unable even to get in the water when the spring began to flow. He was the very picture of helplessness.

Jesus approached him individually and spoke to him privately, asking a question whose answer would seem to be obvious: "Do you want to be made well?" (v. 6). The man's reply reveals what was on his mind: he was frustrated and discouraged. He was within a few feet of the scant relief available to him, and yet it was no benefit to him whatsoever, because when the soothing waters were flowing, he could not get into the pool before being crowded aside by others. It was an exasperating indignity for him, and he was clearly brooding about it when Jesus approached him.

The man perhaps believed that it was important to be first into the pool as soon as the waters were agitated. He wasn't looking for someone to hold his arm to steady and support him while he got into the pool as best he could. Instead, the phrase he used in verse 7 could be literally translated, "I have no one to *cast* me into the pool when the water is stirred up." He may have been hinting that if Jesus was really interested in a lame man's well-being, He should stand by until the waters were stirred again, and then quickly fling the man into the pool!

That was as good as a *yes* answer to Jesus' question, because without another word, Jesus said to him, "Rise, take up your bed and walk" (v. 8). It was practically the same form of expression Jesus had used with the paralytic in Capernaum: three imperatives, all commands the poor man had no ability in himself to obey. But with the command came miraculous power from on high, and *"immediately"* (v. 9) the man's thirty-eight-year-long affliction came to an end. He simply picked up his pallet and walked away. Jesus, meanwhile, quietly blended in with the crowd (v. 13).

In the scope of Jesus' whole ministry, this might have seemed a fairly unremarkable healing. It wasn't accompanied by any sermon or public discourse. Jesus simply spoke privately and very briefly with this one infirm man in a context so crowded that few people, if any, were likely to notice. There was no fanfare prior to the healing, and John's description of the incident gives us no reason to think the man's healing resulted in any public spectacle. Jesus had healed countless people before, and in that light, everything about this incident was more or less routine for the ministry of Jesus.

Except for one detail. John closes verse 9 by noting, "And that day was the Sabbath." At first glance, that may appear to be an incidental background fact. But it is actually the turning point of the narrative, sparking a conflict that will mark yet another escalation of hostility between Jesus and the chief religious leaders of Israel. By the end of this day, their contempt for Him will have been ratcheted up to such a level of pure hatred that from now on they will not rest—or let Him rest—until they have completely eliminated Him.

Remember that matters concerning obedience on the Sabbath were the Pharisees' home turf. Jesus knew full well that they were almost fanatical about it. They had invented all kinds of restrictions for the day of rest, adding their own super-strict rules to Moses' law in the name of tradition. They treated their manmade customs as if they were binding law, equal in authority to the revealed Word of God.

Of course, they did the same thing with all the law's ceremonial precepts, going far beyond what Scripture required. They made every ritual as elaborate and every ordinance as restrictive as possible. They believed this was a pathway to greater holiness. But the Sabbath was a weekly event, the very heartbeat of Israel's religious life and a symbol of theocracy. As such it was a constant reminder that true authority under Moses' law came from God through the priesthood—not by governmental decrees from an earthly king or Caesar. So the high-handed authority the Pharisees claimed over that day was the one great tradition they guarded most fiercely.

They insisted that *everyone* must rigidly observe their

Sabbatarian principles. In Jerusalem especially, the entire population was basically required to observe the Sabbath in the manner of the Pharisees. In Jerusalem, even pagan Roman soldiers showed as much deference as possible to the Pharisees' rules on that one day each week. Ultra-strict Sabbatarian legalism thus became the defining cultural emblem of life and religion in Israel.

Jesus, however, refused to bow to the Pharisees' manmade rules. He broke their Sabbaths openly, repeatedly, and deliberately. He taught that "the Sabbath was made for man, and not man for the Sabbath" (Mark 2:27). He then followed that statement by boldly telling the Pharisees, "Therefore the Son of Man is also Lord of the Sabbath" (v. 28).

The first major conflict over these matters broke out in the wake of this quiet Sabbath healing at the pool of Bethesda. Almost as soon as the healed man picked up his bed (for the first time in thirty-eight years) and began to walk away, he met some religious leaders who accused him of breaking the Sabbath. Before the day was over, Jesus would justify His own breaking of the Pharisees' Sabbath restrictions by saying He is God's Son and therefore perfectly free to do what God Himself does on the Sabbath.

This one incident pretty much determined the issues and set the tone that would dominate Jesus' controversy with the Sanhedrin for the rest of His earthly life. From this day forward, the vast majority of conflicts between Jesus and the Pharisees will involve the question of who truly has authority over the Sabbath. Their Sabbath traditions and His divine authority will thus become the twin issues upon which all the Pharisees' conflicts with Jesus now crystallize. Virtually every public controversy He will have with them from here on will be sparked either by His refusal to bow to their legalism, His claims of equality with God, or both. His clear stance on *both* points of controversy is perfectly summarized in the declaration that *He* is Lord of the Sabbath.

Now observe how this first Sabbath conflict arose.

Not Lawful to Carry Your Bed

No one could walk through Jerusalem carrying *anything* on the Sabbath (much less a cot or stretcher large enough for a grown man) without catching the critical eye of some Pharisee—especially this close to the temple. Predictably, before the formerly disabled man had traveled very far from the pool of Bethesda, a band of religious authorities stopped him and challenged his right to carry his own sickbed on the day of rest. (John refers to the man's interlocutors as "the Jews," which in John's gospel almost always signifies recognized, high-ranking religious authorities. So these men were probably members of the Sanhedrin council.) "It is the Sabbath," they curtly told him; "it is not lawful for you to carry your bed" (John 5:10).

The man explained that he had just received a miraculous healing, and that "He who made me well said to me, 'Take up your bed and walk'" (v. 11).

Do not miss the fact that these religious authorities were more concerned about manmade Sabbath traditions than they were with the well-being of a man who had suffered for such a long time. They were acting like middle-school hall monitors rather than mature human beings. So much for their claims of moral superiority. Even most of the people the Pharisees always looked down on would have responded better than they did. Anyone with an ounce of feeling and a basic sense of humanity would naturally rejoice with the man over his good fortune. Simple curiosity would prompt most of us to ask for more details about what had happened and how such a marvelous healing after so long an affliction had suddenly come to pass. It takes a peculiar brand of hyper-religious self-righteousness for anyone to behave as callously as these Jewish authorities did. They totally ignored the glorious triumph of the healing and demanded to know precisely who had healed him, so that they could take up their grievance with whoever *told* this man it was okay to carry his bed.

But Jesus had already slipped away into the multitudes. The brief encounter at Bethesda had been so unexpected and was all accomplished so quickly that the man had not even had time to find out who it was that healed him.

Jesus Equating Himself with God

Apparently the man was somewhere between Bethesda and the temple when he was stopped and challenged. That would mean he walked only a very short distance before being accused of Sabbath-breaking. A short time later, "Jesus found him in the temple, and said to him, 'See, you have been made well. Sin no more, lest a worse thing come upon you'" (v. 14).

We're not told anything about the spiritual state of this man. Jesus did not declare his sins forgiven, as He had in the case of the paralytic at Capernaum. Nor did Christ comment on the man's faith, as He often did when healing people (e.g., Matthew 9:22; Mark 10:52; Luke 7:50; 17:19). The fact that he was in the temple is the only clue we have that he had any spiritual interest at all.

But the man's faith seems questionable because of how he reacted after meeting Jesus in the temple and discovering the identity of the One who had healed him. If he expressed any praise or thanksgiving—or made any answer to Jesus at all—John doesn't mention it. Instead, the text says, "The man departed" (John 5:15).

He not only departed the presence of Jesus; he went straight to the Jewish authorities who had confronted him and basically turned Jesus in. It's difficult to imagine any noble motive for him to go groveling to the religious leaders. In the worst case, the man was being sinfully self-serving; in the best case, he was being naively stupid. He could not possibly have had any affection for (or relationship with) the Jewish leaders who had challenged him. They would have treated him as unclean prior to his healing, and they *did* treat him with callous disregard immediately afterward. But he wanted no quarrel with them. And he may have had an undue fear of their disapproval, fearing perhaps that they might really stone him. If so, he may have been merely overeager to clear himself of any blame.

On the other hand, he had every reason to know that the religious leaders were extremely angry about the supposed Sabbath violation. When they originally demanded to know who healed him, it must have been patently obvious to him that they were not looking to congratulate Jesus for His benevolence. If he was so intimidated by them and fearful of the repercussions of their displeasure, it is difficult to explain why he would go out of his way to find them again and bring them fresh intelligence about Jesus.

Whatever reason he had for it, the man headed straight for the religious authorities who had accused him, and he reported that Jesus was the one they were seeking. Predictably, they "persecuted Jesus, and sought to kill Him, because He had done these things on the Sabbath" (v. 16). As soon as the man confirmed who had healed him, these religious leaders made a beeline to Jesus and began to accuse and threaten Him with stoning.

Under Moses' law, any deliberate and egregious violation of the Sabbath was grounds for stoning (Exodus 31:14; 35:2). One of the earliest recorded Old Testament stonings involved a violation of the Sabbath (Numbers 15:32–36). So the religious authorities now believed they had a convenient, biblically defensible motive for stoning Jesus. The Sanhedrin had the power of life and death in religious matters, even under Roman rule, and they frequently employed it to deal with cases of wanton blasphemy and deliberate sacrilege. It is unlikely that the Romans would sanction the execution of someone who violated the Sabbath accidentally or in a merely superficial way. (And this case was a misdemeanor by any measure). But if the religious leaders could build a credible case that Jesus was a malicious and chronic blasphemer, they could put Him to death without any serious challenge from Rome.

This incident that began at Bethesda seems to have planted that notion in their minds, and that is why the Sabbath quickly became the central motif in their conflict with Him. It also explains the obvious change in their strategy from here on out.

They became more bold and outspoken in their accusations. They were no longer trying merely to discredit Him; now they were determined to destroy Him. They began watching Him with an especially close scrutiny on the Sabbaths. In fact, after this, whenever Jesus healed on the Sabbath, there were always Pharisees present who would challenge Him.

But even though He knew full well that every such occasion would provoke open conflict with them, Jesus never backed off or abstained from healing openly on the Sabbath. If anything, He seized those opportunities and did His healings as publicly and as conspicuously as possible. Sometimes He announced to the Pharisees beforehand that He intended to work a miracle, practically daring them to condemn the act *before* He did it (cf. Matthew 12:10; Luke 14:3). He did this, of course, not out of any love for contention, but because it was the best way to highlight the error and injustice that was embedded in the Pharisees' system.

As a matter of fact, on the occasion of this very first Sabbath controversy in Jerusalem, Jesus responded to the religious leaders' condemnation by saying something that was practically guaranteed to offend them more than ever. He said simply: "My Father has been working until now, and I have been working" (John 5:17). In other words, God Himself is not bound by any Sabbath restrictions. He continues His labors day and night (Psalm 121:4; Isaiah 27:3). Jesus was claiming the same prerogative for Himself. He is, after all, Lord of the Sabbath. That is a claim that only God incarnate can righteously make.

The religious leaders got the message instantly. They were already insinuating that He ought to be stoned, even before He made that comment. But now their mood took a turn for the worse, and they "sought all the more to kill Him, because He not only broke the Sabbath, but also said that God was His Father, making Himself equal with God" (John 5:18).

He was indeed equating Himself with God. This was the same issue that prompted them to think He was guilty of blasphemy in Capernaum: "Who can forgive sins but God alone?" (Luke 5:21). On that occasion, He had answered with a demonstration of His divine authority. This time He stood resolutely and expounded fearlessly on the ramifications of His own deity in a discourse that runs from John 5:19 through the end of the chapter. The whole discourse is one more example of Jesus' candid straightforwardness. He even included a powerful denunciation of Israel's top religious leaders, including several statements that rebuke them as total unbelievers. ("How can you believe, who receive honor from one another, and do not seek the honor that comes from the only God?"—v. 44.) He closed with a powerful final castigation of their whole system, citing the one source they *claimed* to trust—the books of Moses—as a witness against them: "Do not think that I shall accuse you to the Father; there is one who accuses you—Moses, in whom you trust. For if you believed Moses, you would believe Me; for he wrote about Me. But if you do not believe his writings, how will you believe My words?" (vv. 45–47).

Jesus was not doing any bridge building with the religious establishment here; He was upbraiding them, and none too gently. Rather than tiptoeing around their well-known religious sensibilities and trying to avoid offense, He portrayed them as utterly unregenerate, spiritually lifeless men (v. 40). And He drove His point home repeatedly, with some of the sharpest words possible: "You do not have His word abiding in you" (v. 38); "You do not have the love of God in you" (v. 42); "You do not believe" (vv. 38, 47).

On the other hand, Jesus was not trying to provoke them merely for sport. He told them, "I say these things that you may be saved" (v. 34). The religious leaders of Israel were lost and progressively hardening their hearts against Jesus. They *needed* some harsh words. He would not permit them to ignore Him, or to ignore His truth, under the guise of showing them the kind of deference and public honor they craved from Him.

Might Jesus have averted all further conflict with the Sanhedrin simply by toning down His message a little and holding a cordial colloquy with the Jewish council right here? Could He have softened their opposition from the start by muting His criticisms of them? Is it possible that they would have left Him alone if He had simply shown them the kind of respect they craved in public contexts, reserving His disagreements for private, friendly, face-to-face contexts?

Perhaps.

But the cause of truth would not have been served by that, and the price of compromise with Israel's religious elite would have been the loss of redemption for all sinners. So Jesus was in fact showing the utmost righteousness and grace, even though He was deliberately provoking them.

The Aftermath

The end of Jesus' discourse is also the end of John 5. No further comments are recorded from the Jewish authorities. But they were by no means letting the matter drop.

Jesus returned to Galilee (John 6:1), and the Pharisees' Galilean delegation immediately began to scrutinize Him with extra diligence on the Sabbath. Almost immediately upon His return to Galilee, Jesus' ministry was marked by a series of conflicts with the Pharisees over His repeated failure to observe the Sabbath on their terms.

The first Galilean conflict over the Sabbath occurred when some Pharisees observed Jesus' disciples picking heads of grain as their path took them through a grain field on the Sabbath. According to Luke 6:1, they were merely "passing through" (NASB); they were not out in the fields gleaning. But "His disciples plucked the heads of grain and ate them, rubbing them in their hands."

By the Pharisees' reckoning, the hand-rubbing motion, which separated the wheat from the chaff, technically was a form of winnowing. Thus it was work, prohibited on the Sabbath under their rules. They challenged Jesus; He defended His disciples' actions with a multifaceted argument from the Old Testament.

He pointed out first of all that David had eaten the Tabernacle showbread when he was hungry (Matthew 12:3–4). In that obscure Old Testament incident (1 Samuel 21:3–6), David and his men were desperately hungry, and they sought rest and refuge near the Tabernacle. The showbread on the altar had just been replaced with fresh bread (v. 6). Even after being retired from the altar, the older showbread was deemed holy and normally reserved only for the priests. But David asked for the bread anyway, pointing out that his men were ceremonially clean (v. 5) and the bread was technically now common. So the priest complied and gave him the bread.

Jesus cited that as proof that *works of necessity and acts of mercy* override the strict requirements of ceremonial law, and thus such works may be done on the Sabbath. As further evidence, He pointed out that priests in the temple *must* work on the Sabbath (Matthew 12:5).

Quoting Hosea 6:6, He then said, "If you had known what this means, 'I desire mercy and not sacrifice,' you would not have condemned the guiltless" (Matthew 12:7). He was making a clear distinction between the law's moral significance ("mercy") and its ceremonial features ("sacrifice"), and suggesting that the moral intent of the law always trumps picayune ceremonial technicalities. That, of course, is the same lesson He was pointing to in David's eating of the showbread.

This was the occasion when He made those two definitive statements explaining why He refused to bow to the Pharisees' Sabbath legalism: "The Sabbath was made for man, and not man for the Sabbath. Therefore the Son of Man is also Lord of the Sabbath" (Mark 2:27–28).

Filled with Rage

Shortly after that ("on another Sabbath"—Luke 6:6), He healed a man with a withered hand in a synagogue where He had gone to teach. Luke says plainly, "The scribes and the Pharisees were watching Him closely to see if He healed on the Sabbath, so that they might find reason to accuse Him. But He knew what they were thinking, and He said to the man with the withered hand, 'Get up and come forward!'" (vv. 7–8 NASB).

Once again Jesus deliberately did something He knew would cause friction. Fully aware that the Pharisees were watching Him closely and that they would be deeply offended if He healed this man on the Sabbath, Jesus brought the man to the front of the synagogue and made the healing as public as He could. He even preceded the healing by openly challenging the Pharisees' error. "I will ask you one thing," He said. "Is it lawful on the Sabbath to do good or to do evil, to save life or to destroy?" (v. 9). Luke suggests that Jesus then made deliberate eye contact with each of His ecclesiastical adversaries just before He healed the man: "When He had looked around at them all, He said to the man, 'Stretch out your hand'" (v. 10).

It was one of those undeniable, divinely empowered miracles involving the power of creation. The arm that had been shriveled and physically deformed was suddenly made whole! Who could doubt that this was the power of God on display?

But the Pharisees in the audience were unmoved by the miracle. Instead, they were aroused with fury against Jesus. "They were filled with rage" (v. 11).

What did Jesus hope to accomplish by doing something He knew would infuriate the Pharisees? Why would He not rather take them aside and try to correct them privately? Why would He not try to be a bridge builder rather than a wall builder? Why would He purposely provoke strife rather than trying to make peace? And if it was necessary to set the Pharisees straight on their views about the Sabbath, would it not be better to keep that conflict between Him and them?

Why would He provoke these men in front of a crowd of lay-people in a place of worship? Why pick *this* fight over an issue that was so dear to them?

But again, Jesus was not provoking the Pharisees for sport or for pleasure. Moreover, this dispute was not merely about who had the right view of *ceremony*. The bigger, underlying issue was still the principle of justification and how sinners can be made right with God. Justification is not earned by merit, nor is it gained through rituals. True righteousness cannot be earned by human works, but forgiveness and full justification are freely given to those who believe.

In other words, the difference between Jesus and the Pharisees was not that they had differing customs regarding how to observe the Sabbath; it was that they held contradictory views on the way of salvation. That truth was too important to bury under the blanket of an artificial civility. The gospel must be defended against lies and false teaching, and the fact that gospel truth often offends even the most distinguished religious people is *never* a reason for trying to tame the message or tone it down. Jesus Himself is our model for that.

The scribes and Pharisees in Luke 6 were so deeply offended by Jesus that they gathered afterward "and discussed with one another what they might do to Jesus" (v. 11). Mark 3:6 says they "went out and immediately plotted with the Herodians against Him, how they might destroy Him."

The religious authorities' course was set, and their hearts were steadily hardening. Their determination to see Jesus put to death had now developed into a full-fledged plot. Many more conflicts were yet to come, and neither Jesus nor His religious adversaries showed any signs of backing down.

Why mild? Of all the epithets that could be applied to Christ this seems one of the least appropriate. . . . Jesus Christ might well be called "meek," in the sense of being selfless and humble and utterly devoted to what He considered right, whatever the personal cost; but "mild," never!

—J. B. Phillips

Six

HARD PREACHING

_____

Does this offend you?
JOHN 6:61

Jesus' conflict with the Pharisees was not a quiet disagreement carried on in a secret corner. Nor did Jesus Himself seek to soften the public aspect of His running feud with the religious leaders. He had none of the scruples about propriety and politeness that are so prevalent in public theological discourse nowadays. On the contrary, Jesus' preaching was probably the most important aspect of His relentless polemic against the leaders of the Jewish religious establishment and the institutionalized hypocrisy they embodied. It was clear to everyone that the Pharisees' teaching was one of His primary targets, whether He was giving a discourse for His disciples' benefit or preaching to vast multitudes.

As a matter of fact, the whole theme of the Sermon on the Mount (Luke 6; Matthew 5–7) was a critique of the Pharisees' religion. He condemned their doctrine, their phony approach to practical holiness, their pedantic style of Scripture twisting, and their smug overconfidence. The Bread of Life discourse (John 6) likewise provoked such a conflict with the Pharisees that most of Jesus' own followers became seriously uncomfortable. Many of them stopped following Him after that.

The Sermon on the Mount

Jesus' best-known and longest recorded sermon comes after the halfway point in a timeline of His public ministry. Just before preaching the sermon, Jesus went to the top of a nearby mountain and spent the entire night in prayer (Luke 6:12). It was clear that something remarkable was happening on the mountain that day, because a great multitude of disciples were awaiting Jesus when He came down.

Jesus' sermon begins with the Beatitudes—that familiar series of blessings. There are eight of them in Matthew's account, and combined, they describe the true nature of saving faith.

> Blessed are the poor in spirit, for theirs is the kingdom of heaven. Blessed are those who mourn, for they shall be comforted. Blessed are the meek, for they shall inherit the earth. Blessed are those who hunger and thirst for righteousness, for they shall be filled. Blessed are the merciful, for they shall obtain mercy. Blessed are the pure in heart, for they shall see God. Blessed are the peacemakers, for they shall be called sons of God. Blessed are those who are persecuted for righteousness' sake, for theirs is the kingdom of heaven.

> Blessed are you when they revile and persecute you, and say all kinds of evil against you falsely for My sake. Rejoice and be exceedingly glad, for great is your reward in heaven, for so they persecuted the prophets who were before you.
>
> **(Matthew 5:3–12)**

The "poor in spirit" (v. 3) are those who know they have no spiritual resources of their own. "Those who mourn" (v. 4) are repentant people, truly sorrowful over their own sin. "The meek" (v. 5) are those who truly fear God and know their own unworthiness in light of His holiness. "Those who hunger and thirst for righteousness" (v. 6) are those who, having turned from sin, yearn for what God loves instead. Those four beatitudes are all *inward qualities* of authentic faith. They describe how the believer sees himself before God: poor, sorrowful, meek, and hungry.

The final four beatitudes describe the *outward manifestations* of those qualities. They describe what the authentic Christian should look like to an objective observer. "The merciful" (v. 7) are those who, as beneficiaries of God's grace, extend grace to others. "The pure in heart" (v. 8) describes people whose thoughts and actions are characterized by holiness. "The peacemakers" (v. 9) speaks mainly of those who spread the message of "peace with God through our Lord Jesus Christ" (Romans 5:1)—which is the only true and lasting peace. And obviously, "those who are persecuted for righteousness' sake" (Matthew 5:10) are citizens of Christ's kingdom who suffer because of their affiliation with Him and their faithfulness to Him. The world hates them because it hates Him (John 15:18; 1 John 3:1, 13).

Jesus could hardly have devised a list of virtues more at odds with the style of religion that dominated that culture.

Consider this: the Pharisees as a group stood on the wrong side of every one of those lines in the sand. Spiritual self-sufficiency defined their whole system. They refused to acknowledge their sin, much less mourn over it. Far from being meek, they were the very embodiment of stubborn, overbearing self-assertiveness. They didn't hunger and thirst for righteousness; they actually thought they had perfected it. They were not merciful but specialized in "bind[ing] heavy burdens, hard to bear, and lay[ing] them on men's shoulders; but they themselves [would] not move them with one of their fingers" (Matthew 23:4). Their hearts were impure, not pure, and Jesus confronted them about that regularly (Matthew 23:27). They were spiritual troublemakers, not peacemakers. And above all, they were the quintessential persecutors of the righteous. Their dealings with Jesus were already beginning to make that clear.

The Beatitudes were a rebuke to the Pharisees' whole system. Any Pharisees who might have been in the crowd listening to the sermon would certainly have felt personally attacked and publicly humiliated. And if there were any doubt of His intentions, proof that Jesus *meant* to chide them is seen throughout the rest of the sermon. In fact, the central message of the Sermon on the Mount is summed up in Matthew 5:20: "I say to you, that unless your righteousness exceeds the righteousness of the scribes and Pharisees, you will by no means enter the kingdom of heaven." The sermon is a sustained critique of their whole religious system. The Beatitudes are merely an introduction, contrasting the spirit of authentic faith with the hypocrisy of pharisaical self-righteousness.

93

You Have Heard . . . But I Say

After the Beatitudes, Jesus goes straight into an extended discourse on the true meaning of Old Testament law. The rest of Matthew 5 is a systematic, point-by-point critique of the Pharisees' interpretation of Moses' law. Jesus is correcting some of their representative errors.

Some commentators have suggested that Jesus is altering or expanding the moral requirements of Moses' law for a new dispensation. Jesus Himself said otherwise: "Do not think that I came to destroy the Law or the Prophets. I did not come to destroy but to fulfill. For assuredly, I say to you, till heaven and earth pass away, one jot or one tittle will by no means pass from the law till all is fulfilled" (vv. 17–18).

Indeed, every principle Jesus used to refute the Pharisees' interpretation of the law was already either stated or plainly implied in the Old Testament. More on that shortly.

But what is most important to notice here is that Jesus deliberately sets His description of authentic righteousness *against* the religion of the Pharisees. The brunt of the sermon is a jeremiad against their unique brand of hypocrisy. That is the singular theme that ties the whole sermon together.

Furthermore, when He singled out these specific misunderstandings of Moses' law, Jesus was clearly impugning the Pharisees' pet doctrines. Everyone in the crowd understood that. Jesus made no effort to make the dichotomy subtle or to outline His differences with them in a delicate fashion. He even mentioned the Pharisees by name and expressly stated that their righteousness was inadequate—lest there be any ambiguity about *whose* doctrine He was refuting.

Immediately after saying, "Unless your righteousness exceeds the righteousness of the scribes and Pharisees, you will by no means enter the kingdom of heaven" (v. 20), He began dismantling their whole system. He attacked their method of interpreting Scripture, their means of applying the law, their notions of guilt and merit, their infatuation with ceremonial minutiae, and their love for moral and doctrinal casuistry.

The major arguments in this section of the sermon are structured in a way that contrasts the Pharisees' interpretation of the law with the law's real meaning, as expounded by Christ: "You have *heard* that it was said to those of old . . . . But *I* say to you . . ." Six times in the second half of Matthew 5, Jesus used that formula or a variation of it (vv. 21–22, 26–28, 31–32, 33–34, 38–39, 43–44). When He spoke of what "you have heard," He was describing the Pharisees' teaching. And in each case, He refuted it.

Again, He was not changing or expanding the law's moral requirements; He was simply reaffirming what the law always meant. "Your commandment is exceedingly broad," David said, as he meditated on the law (Psalm 119:96). The meaning of the Ten Commandments is not exhausted by the wooden literal sense of the words. Jesus says, for example, that the sixth commandment forbids not only literal acts of murder, but murderous attitudes as well—including undue anger, abusive speech, and an unforgiving spirit (Matthew 5:22–25). The seventh commandment forbids not merely acts of adultery, but even an adulterous heart (v. 28). The command to love your neighbor applies not only to friendly neighbors, but also to those who are our enemies (v. 44).

Superficial readers are sometimes inclined to think Jesus

was modifying or raising the bar on the standard of Moses' law. After all, He quoted directly from the sixth and seventh commandments (vv. 21, 27), and He cited the Old Testament principle known as *lex talionis* ("an eye for an eye and a tooth for a tooth"—v. 38; cf. Exodus 21:24, Leviticus 24:20, and Deuteronomy 19:21). Then He followed those quotations with "But I say to you . . ." To a casual listener, it might actually sound as if He were changing the law itself, or making a new law that stood in contrast to what the Old Testament had always taught. But remember: Jesus Himself unequivocally denied that notion in verses 17–18.

Instead, what Jesus is doing in this portion of the sermon is unpacking the true and full meaning of the law as it was originally intended—especially in contrast to the limited, narrow, and woodenly literal approach of the Pharisees. Their hermeneutic (the method by which they interpreted Scripture) was laden with sophistry. They could expound for hours on the law's invisible fine points while inventing technical twists and turns to make exceptions to some of the law's most important moral precepts.

For example, the fifth commandment is clear enough: "Honor your father and your mother" (Exodus 20:12). But the Pharisees had a custom whereby "if a man says to his father or mother, 'Whatever profit you might have received from me is Corban'—(that is, a gift to God), then [the Pharisees] no longer let him do anything for his father or his mother" (Mark 7:11–12). In fact, if someone had thus pledged his inheritance to God and then used any of his resources to care for his parents in their old age, the Pharisees would deem that act of charity a sacrilege, because it was a violation of the *Corban* vow. Jesus told them, "[You have made] the word of God of no effect through your tradition which you have handed down. *And many such things you do*" (v. 13).

That was precisely the kind of hermeneutical tomfoolery Jesus was correcting in the Sermon on the Mount. The Pharisees were fierce in their opposition to sins that others could see, but they tended to excuse or absolve themselves of whatever wickedness was hidden in the privacy of their own hearts. That was the error that lay at the root of all the Pharisees' errors. It was how they justified all their hypocrisy.

And as for the Old Testament's eye-for-an-eye rule, the context of Exodus 21:24–25, where that standard was given, shows that it was a principle designed to *limit* penalties assessed in civil and criminal court cases. It was never supposed to authorize private retaliation for petty insults and personal infractions. It was a principle that kept the *legal* system in check (cf. Exodus 21:1), not a rule designed to unleash neighbor against neighbor in a back-and-forth war of attacks and counterattacks. But the Pharisees had basically turned it into that. Personal vengeance poisoned the social atmosphere of Israel, and the religious leaders justified it by an appeal to Moses. Jesus said that was a total misuse and abuse of Moses' law.

Clearly, Jesus was in no way expressing disagreement with Moses' law or amending its moral content. He was simply refuting the Pharisees' misconstrued teaching about the law's moral precepts.

Any Pharisee who may have been in the audience for the Sermon on the Mount would have understood Jesus' message plainly enough: their righteousness, with all its stress on pomp and circumcision, simply did not meet the divine standard.

They weren't really any better than the tax collectors. And God would *not* accept their imperfect righteousness. Jesus was as direct as possible about that. He could hardly have spoken any words that would hit them harder. According to Him, their religion was utterly worthless.

Do Not Be Like the Hypocrites

Jesus was far from finished with the point. Practically all of Matthew 6 continues with a hammering, point-by-point critique of the most visible traits of Pharisaism. The sermon was not delivered with chapter divisions, of course, so it's important to keep in mind that the whole catalogue of hypocrisies Jesus attacks in chapter 6 comes hard on the heels of His critique of the Pharisees' misinterpretation of the law in chapter 5. In a way, chapter 5 was merely a warmup for what follows, and chapter 6 is just further development of the key proposition set forth in 5:20: "Unless your righteousness exceeds the righteousness of the scribes and Pharisees, you will by no means enter the kingdom of heaven."

Incidentally, even if Jesus had not specifically named the Pharisees, every person in His audience would have known exactly whom He was talking about, if only from the roster of hypocrisies He outlined in chapter 6. Those were the main badges of the Pharisees' religion. A Pharisee's broad phylacteries and the jumbo-sized tassels on the four corners of his robe (cf. Deuteronomy 22:12) were fitting metaphors for the many ways the Pharisees made their religiosity as ostentatious as possible. They were almost constitutionally incapable of doing any act of charity or piety without making a tawdry public display out of it in the process.

That is precisely what most of Matthew 6 is about. Jesus was contrasting the religious exhibitionism of the Pharisees with the authentic faith He had described in the Beatitudes. Faith has its primary impact on the heart of the believer. The Pharisees' religion, by contrast, was mainly for show, "to be seen" by others (Matthew 6:1). Since that was the only reward that really mattered to them, that was all the reward they would get (v. 2).

Jesus depicted them as sounding a trumpet before them when they did charitable deeds (v. 2). There's no record in any of the literature from that era where anyone *actually* held a parade with trumpets when they did their alms. Our Lord was painting a colorful word picture, actually making a humorous parody of the Pharisees' spiritual flamboyance. He was using sanctified mockery to expose the silliness of their system.

He went on to rebuke the hypocrisy of loud, long public prayers (another specialty of the Pharisees), again saying that the earthly attention such a practice garners is its only reward (v. 5). It was at this point that He first gave the model prayer that has become known as the Lord's Prayer. That prayer's brevity, simplicity, and Godward focus set it apart from the Pharisees' style of praying.

Next, He turned to the subject of fasting, a practice that was badly abused by the Pharisees. Jesus described how they exploited even this highly personal spiritual discipline as a means of billboarding their own righteousness: "They disfigure their faces that they may appear to men to be fasting" (Matthew 6:16). Specifically, they put on "a sad countenance," ostensibly as a token of solemn devotion and grim self-sacrifice. But in reality it was all a charade—a thin, worn-out veneer that barely covered their totally selfish motives. Of course, legitimate fasting is supposed to be a means of helping us set aside worldly concerns in order to focus on prayer and spiritual things. The Pharisees instead had turned their fasting into another means of parading their piety in public, proving once more that they could not have cared less about heavenly things. What they really cared for was worldly applause. All their fasting had the exact opposite effect of what a fast should do; it drew attention to them, rather than eliminating things that distract. Jesus exposed the hypocrisy of it.

The rest of Matthew 6 (verses 19–34) is a short lesson on the importance of maintaining a heavenly perspective. It sets forth the same principle the apostle Paul would later summarize in Colossians 3:2: "Set your mind on things above, not on things on the earth." Jesus includes a corresponding warning against being consumed with earthly cares. In this section of the Sermon on the Mount, He talks about the proper use of our financial resources (vv. 19–24). He also addresses the sin of worry (vv. 25–34). Those who fret about the future, according to Jesus, manifest a lack of trust in God and a skewed sense of priorities.

All of this, too, is merely a continuation of Jesus' diatribe against the Pharisees' approach to religion. The attitude Jesus was condemning was an inevitable fruit of the Pharisees' infatuation with external things. It colored all their thoughts—making them pathologically superficial; giving them a carnal, earthbound perspective and keeping them from truly trusting God. That's why they (and their disciples) were obsessed with wealth and asphyxiated with worry. This is clearly seen in the rationale underlying their whole conspiracy against Jesus. All their animosity toward Him was driven by a fear that if He came to power as Messiah, they would lose their status, their means of wealth, and all their earthly advantages (John 11:48). Despite all their pious pretenses, those things meant more to them than righteousness. So when Jesus says, "Seek first the kingdom of God and His righteousness, and all these things shall be added to you," He was teaching yet another truth that directly assaulted the Pharisees' value system (Matthew 6:33).

Bad Trees, Bad Fruit

Matthew 7 continues and concludes the Sermon on the Mount with some of Jesus' most devastating denunciations of Pharisaism so far. The chapter starts with an assault on self-righteous judgmentalism. (The Pharisees were masters at that.) Jesus conjures up the ludicrous imagery of someone with a large piece of wood embedded in his eye trying to remove a tiny speck from someone else's eye (vv. 1–5). This was another verbal caricature about the Pharisees, who would do things like criticizing the disciples for rubbing a handful of grain on the Sabbath (Matthew 12:2), but whose own hearts and minds were private dens of iniquity, given over to all kinds of evil thinking (v. 34).

It is crucial to understand verse 1 properly. "Judge not, that you be not judged" is not a blanket condemnation of all kinds of judgment—just the hypocritical, superficial, and misguided kinds of judgments the Pharisees made. The context makes clear that this is a call for charity and generosity in the judgments we make, "For with what judgment you judge, you will be judged; and with the measure you use, it will be measured back to you" (v. 2). It is often necessary to make judgments, and when we do, we must "not judge according to appearance, but judge with righteous judgment" (John 7:24).

Jesus' own words make it clear that He expects us to make discerning judgments, because He goes on to say, "Do not give what is holy to the dogs; nor cast your pearls before swine" (v. 6). "Swine" and "dogs" in that verse refer to people who are chronically antagonistic to the gospel—those whose predictable response to sacred things is that they will "trample them under their feet, and turn and tear [the messenger] in pieces" (v. 6). Obviously, in order to obey that command, we have to know who the swine and dogs are. So an underlying assumption is that we *must* judge carefully and biblically.

But what is most intriguing here is that Jesus was clearly alluding to the Pharisees and others like them, not to the Gentiles and moral pariahs who were normally labeled "swine" and "dogs" by Israel's religious elite. Pigs and dogs were unclean animals under Old Testament law, of course. So swine were never raised by Jewish people as domesticated livestock. Dogs were not kept as house pets. Both species were generally thought of only as wild, bad-tempered scavengers. Naturally, those labels carried a very strong connotation of uncleanness and inhumanity. They were normally applied only to society's lowest outcasts and untouchables.

Remember, however, that Jesus had a vibrant ministry among the very people who were usually on the receiving end of such epithets. That is why the Pharisees derisively called

Him "a glutton and a winebibber, a friend of tax collectors and sinners" (Luke 7:34). Given the context of the Sermon on the Mount and Jesus' relentless assault on the Pharisees' hypocrisy and religious exhibitionism, it is clear whom He had in mind when He forbade casting pearls before swine. It was not the penitent publicans and sinners to whom He regularly showed mercy.

Jesus Himself modeled the kind of discretion He is calling for here. He regularly "[hid] things from the wise and prudent and revealed them to babes" (Luke 10:21). In other words, to humble and repentant people, He always gave more and taught more. But He deliberately concealed truth from arrogant and self-righteous people, "so that 'seeing they may see and not perceive, and hearing they may hear and not understand'" (Mark 4:12). His parables served this very purpose: they obscured the truth from people whose hearts had grown dull and whose spiritual ears were hard of hearing (Matthew 13:15). He did not give sacred things to dogs or cast His pearls before swine.

In short, swine and dogs represent the spiritual antitheses of "those who hunger and thirst for righteousness" (Matthew 5:6). The former are puffed up with self and predisposed to reject *any* truth that does not fit their agenda. They will then turn against the messenger and rend him or her in pieces. That is precisely what the Pharisees and their coconspirators were already poised to do to Jesus.

The Pharisees were living examples of the false prophets Jesus mentions in Matthew 7:15. They "come to you in sheep's clothing, but inwardly they are ravenous wolves." That verse is, of course, a generic description of *all* false prophets in all ages, but the religious elite of Israel epitomized everything He was talking about. That fact was surely not lost on them, or on the general audience.

"You will know them by their fruits," Jesus said (v. 16). The imagery of bad trees with bad fruit had special significance for the Pharisees. Some Pharisees and Sadducees had come to John the Baptist not many months before this. Apparently they saw how popular John was, and they wanted the admiration of his followers. John called them the offspring of vipers and told them to "bear fruits worthy of repentance" (Matthew 3:7–8). Then he added, "Even now the ax is laid to the root of the trees. Therefore every tree which does not bear good fruit is cut down and thrown into the fire" (v. 10)—and began to prophesy about Jesus. Now, in wrapping up His Sermon on the Mount, Jesus employed the very same imagery, and even quoted John the Baptist's exact words: "Every good tree bears good fruit, but a bad tree bears bad fruit. A good tree cannot bear bad fruit, nor can a bad tree bear good fruit. *Every tree that does not bear good fruit is cut down and thrown into the fire.* Therefore by their fruits you will know them" (7:17–20).

Those were strong words of condemnation, and though Jesus' admonition was not limited to religious leaders only, no one could possibly miss the fact that Jesus was treading directly on the toes of the Pharisees and Sadducees.

A Message for the Masses

Nevertheless, it would be wrong to conclude that the Sermon on the Mount was only—or even *mainly*—preached for the benefit of Israel's hypocritical religious leaders. While the

Pharisees and Sadducees epitomized the hypocrisy and self-righteousness Jesus targeted, they were by no means the only ones with whom He was pleading. He was speaking to everyone on the broad road. His description of the judgment that awaits at the end of that road is chilling:

> Not everyone who says to Me, "Lord, Lord," shall enter the kingdom of heaven, but he who does the will of My Father in heaven. Many will say to Me in that day, "Lord, Lord, have we not prophesied in Your name, cast out demons in Your name, and done many wonders in Your name?" And then I will declare to them, "I never knew you; depart from Me, you who practice lawlessness!"
>
> Therefore whoever hears these sayings of Mine, and does them, I will liken him to a wise man who built his house on the rock: and the rain descended, the floods came, and the winds blew and beat on that house; and it did not fall, for it was founded on the rock.
>
> But everyone who hears these sayings of Mine, and does not do them, will be like a foolish man who built his house on the sand: and the rain descended, the floods came, and the winds blew and beat on that house; and it fell. And great was its fall.
>
> **(Matthew 7:21–27)**

The word *many* echoes through the passage. *Many* go in by the wide gate onto the broad road (v. 13). *Many* will say "Have we not . . . done *many* wonders?" (v. 22). But notice:

It's not merely Pharisees and Sadducees who will try to argue at the judgment seat that their works ought to be sufficient to get them into heaven. Jesus is describing people who profess to be Christians. They call Jesus "Lord, Lord." They claim to have done mighty works *in His name.* But He sends them away with these soul-shattering words: "I never knew you; depart from Me" (v. 23).

So it turns out the Sermon on the Mount is not a message just for the Pharisees, even though Jesus attacked their beliefs from the start of the sermon through its conclusion. The underlying message is chiefly for disciples, and it is a warning to them, lest they fall into the very same errors that turned the Pharisees' religion into a monstrosity that was odious to God and made them hostile to the truth.

More Hard Words for Disciples

Those final words from the Sermon on the Mount left people breathless. They "were astonished at His teaching, for He taught them as one having authority, and not as the scribes" (vv. 28–29).

The Pharisees could not teach without citing this or that rabbi and resting on the pedigree of centuries-long traditions. Their religion was academic in practically every sense of that word. And to many of them, teaching was just another opportunity to seek praise from men—by showing off their erudition. They took great pride in citing as many sources as possible, carefully footnoting their sermons. They were more concerned with what others said about the law than they were with what the law itself actually taught. They had thus learned the law without ever really listening to it (cf. Galatians 4:21).

Jesus, by contrast, spoke as one who *has* authority, because He does. He is God, and His style of delivery reflected that. If He cited religious scholars at all, it was to refute them. He wasn't inviting an exchange of opinions, giving an academic lecture, or looking for common cause with the religious leaders of the land; He was declaring the Word of God *against* them.

That was every bit as shocking in Jesus' culture as it would be in ours. Don't miss the real import of verses 28–29. People weren't exactly delighted by Jesus' approach. They were "astonished" at first. Soon they would grow angry.

For His part, the more Jesus preached to the same crowds again and again, the more His messages were filled with rebukes and urgent pleas for their repentance. He was not impressed with the size or enthusiasm of large crowds. He was not interested in accumulating the kind of disciples whose main concern was for what they might get out of the relationship. He never upholstered His message to make it more cushy for popular opinion, and He never turned down the rhetorical heat in order to keep the congregation as comfortable as possible. If anything, His approach was the exact opposite. He seemed to do everything He could to disquiet the merely curious who were unconverted. They absolutely loved it when He did miracles. He rebuked them for that, and He made sure they could not ignore His *message.*

The site where Jesus preached the Sermon on the Mount was situated somewhere between the villages of Capernaum and Chorazin. Not many days after He gave that sermon,

Jesus preached another sermon at or very near the same spot. Matthew 11:20–24 describes what happened:

> Then He began to rebuke the cities in which most of His mighty works had been done, because they did not repent: "Woe to you, Chorazin! Woe to you, Bethsaida! For if the mighty works which were done in you had been done in Tyre and Sidon, they would have repented long ago in sackcloth and ashes. But I say to you, it will be more tolerable for Tyre and Sidon in the day of judgment than for you. And you, Capernaum, who are exalted to heaven, will be brought down to Hades; for if the mighty works which were done in you had been done in Sodom, it would have remained until this day. But I say to you that it shall be more tolerable for the land of Sodom in the day of judgment than for you."

Harsh words, indeed. That reproof signaled another major change in Jesus' public ministry. From that time forth, He moved around Galilee more and focused more on private instruction for a steadily decreasing circle of the most devoted disciples. His subsequent public discourses tended to be more urgent and more severe.

The Bread of Life Discourse

John 6 contains one of the best-known examples of Jesus' hard preaching. The chapter also chronicles the rejection of Jesus by a large number of people who had once followed Him closely enough to be numbered among His disciples. When His message began to sound harsh and offensive, they turned away in droves.

The beginning of that chapter features the feeding of the five thousand. Jesus was ministering near the shore of Galilee (v. 1) to that "great multitude" (vv. 2, 5) of *at least* five thousand people (v. 10). Mark 3:7–8 says, "A large multitude from Galilee followed, and also from Judea, and from Jerusalem, and from Idumea, and beyond the Jordan, and the vicinity of Tyre and Sidon, a great number of people heard about everything that He was doing and came to Him" (NASB). They must have filled every available place of lodging in Capernaum, Chorazin, Bethsaida, and all the surrounding villages. Those who could not find lodging would find places to camp in the region. All of Galilee was abuzz with activity and talk about Jesus.

That is the picture we see at the start of John 6: enthusiastic multitudes coming to see Jesus from faraway regions, all of them excited about His miracles and devoted enough to come and learn from Him in person. The natural human response would be to take this as a wholly positive sign that Jesus was making a major impact on His culture. He was accumulating followers who would be able to take His message back to their own communities. It looked for all the world like it might be the start of a grassroots movement that had the potential to influence the whole world.

Indeed, it was that. But the big picture was not nearly as positive as it appeared at first glance. Jesus' strategy was not to accumulate crowds of thousands whose main interest was seeing miracles. His energies were focused on training eleven disciples who were the backbone of His entire plan. *They* were the key to the church's eventual worldwide expansion. As for the crowds, there were no doubt many true believers among them, as well as many halfhearted hangers-on. Jesus fearlessly and unapologetically gave them all the message they needed to hear—in unvarnished terms. He was impossible to ignore, and the truth He taught was impossible to miss.

John 6 is a record of how all the public goodwill generated by Jesus' miracles gave way to anger and outrage because of the message He proclaimed. The massive crowds dwindled to virtually nothing in the course of a few verses.

The setting is important. Jesus had fed the multitudes somewhere on the eastern shore of Galilee, then (walking on water in stormy weather) had gone back to Capernaum (on the north shore) to get away from the passionate crowd. When word reached Tiberias (on the western shore) about the feeding of the five thousand, many more people came looking for Jesus, hoping for a repeat performance.

They found Jesus in Capernaum (John 6:24–25; cf. v. 59). His message began with a rebuke of their motives: "Most assuredly, I say to you, you seek Me, not because you saw the signs, but because you ate of the loaves and were filled. Do not labor for the food which perishes, but for the food which endures to everlasting life, which the Son of Man will give you, because God the Father has set His seal on Him" (vv. 26–27).

He wanted to talk to them about spiritual things; they were interested mainly in lunch. They began to bargain. They would hear what He had to say *if* He would give them food. As if to put a spiritual spin on the demand, they pointed out that, after all, the manna of Moses' day was literal food that could be eaten: "Our fathers ate the manna in the desert; as it is written, 'He gave them bread from heaven to eat'" (v. 31).

Jesus continued to speak of a different kind of food from heaven—"*True* bread." But, He said, the bread that gives life is a Person, not an edible substance that could be kept in a jar like manna: "For the bread of God is He who comes down from heaven and gives life to the world" (v. 33).

They were still looking for lunch—still seeking a way to feed their physical appetites—when they said, "Lord, give us this bread always" (v. 34).

The back-and-forth dialogue makes a frustrating study in misunderstanding and spiritual blindness. The voices from the crowd were demanding literal food; Jesus was speaking of something infinitely more important. But they would not see it. There was clearly a tone of testiness and arrogance in their repeated demands (v. 30). It was also obvious that they would not be satisfied with a single encore of the previous day's miracle. "Give us this bread *always*."

Jesus certainly *could* have given them food (or anything else they wanted) whenever they wanted. But He was not there to discuss the lunch menu with them, much less barter for their faith by doing miracles on demand. He was going to talk to them about spiritual things. So He said plainly: "I am the bread of life" (v. 35).

That statement instantly brought murmuring protests from the religious leaders in the crowd. They saw clearly that He was claiming to be more than a mere man. They "complained about Him, because He said, 'I am the bread which came down from heaven.' And they said, 'Is not this Jesus, the son of Joseph, whose father and mother we know?

How is it then that He says, 'I have come down from heaven'?" (vv. 41–42).

Jesus met their disapproval head-on: "Do not murmur among yourselves. I am the bread of life" (vv. 43, 48). It ought to have been perfectly clear that He was speaking of *spiritual* nourishment and *spiritual* life, because He also said, "He who believes in Me has everlasting life" (v. 47). He was giving them the very heart of gospel truth, if they had spiritual ears to hear.

He even explained why the true bread of life is superior to Moses' manna: "Your fathers ate the manna in the wilderness, and are dead. This is the bread which comes down from heaven, that one may eat of it and not die" (vv. 49–50). So this bread could give them spiritual life instead of mere physical nourishment, and the bread was Christ Himself. He was clearly explaining a profound spiritual reality, not describing literal food to be ingested by mouth.

John the Baptist had publicly testified that Jesus was the Lamb of God to take away the sin of the world. Jesus' words echoed that prophecy: "The bread that I shall give is My flesh, which I shall give for the life of the world" (v. 51). The words are full of paschal imagery, revealing Christ as the fulfillment of everything the sacrificial system signified. Just as the symbolic Passover lamb was a feast designed to be eaten, Christ (the *true* Paschal Lamb) was a spiritual banquet to be received by faith. He was the fulfillment of everything the manna and the Passover feast symbolized, and more.

If the multitudes had shown the least bit of interest in hearing the truth, they would have sought clarification of what they did not understand. Jesus was clearly speaking to them about spiritual realities. From the beginning of this increasingly contentious conversation, they had resisted that and clamored for a free lunch instead. Now they were incapable of thinking in other than literal terms.

"The Jews therefore quarreled among themselves, saying, 'How can this Man give us His flesh to eat?'" (v. 52). Remember that John regularly uses the expression "the Jews" to signify the hostile religious leaders. They were apparently at the head of this crowd.

Notice that Jesus did not stop them at that point and say, "No, you misunderstand. Let Me explain what I mean." They had shown no interest in understanding Him, so He persisted with His difficult analogy. In fact, He pressed the metaphor even harder this time:

> Most assuredly, I say to you, unless you eat the flesh
> of the Son of Man and drink His blood, you have no
> life in you. Whoever eats My flesh and drinks My
> blood has eternal life, and I will raise him up at the
> last day. For My flesh is food indeed, and My blood
> is drink indeed. He who eats My flesh and drinks My
> blood abides in Me, and I in him.
>
> **(vv. 53–56)**

Four times in quick succession He spoke of not only eating His flesh, but also drinking His blood.

The symbolic meaning of eating His flesh might have been somewhat transparent to anyone who remembered that the Messiah was the sacrificial lamb who would take away the sin of the world. But when He spoke of drinking His blood, He was using language guaranteed to offend His Jewish audience.

The consumption of blood of any kind was deemed grossly unclean under Old Testament law. "You shall not eat the blood of any flesh, for the life of all flesh is its blood. Whoever eats it shall be cut off" (Leviticus 17:14).

The clearer Jesus made it that He was speaking figuratively about spiritual life and spiritual nourishment, the angrier the contrarians became, and the more offensive His words sounded—especially to the Jewish leaders who considered themselves guardians of public piety and ceremonial purity. Even some of Jesus' own disciples began to whisper among themselves, "This is a hard saying; who can understand it?" (v. 60).

Jesus, knowing full well what they were thinking, simply said, "Does this offend you? What then if you should see the Son of Man ascend where He was before? It is the Spirit who gives life; the flesh profits nothing. The words that I speak to you are spirit, and they are life. But there are some of you who do not believe" (vv. 61–64). Thus He declared plainly that He was using spiritual words to speak of spiritual things. He offered no exegesis of His symbolism and no clarification for the benefit of those who had already become angry with Him. Their failure to grasp His meaning was a fruit of their own unbelief.

That was the end of the discourse. Jesus punctuated it with these words: "Therefore I have said to you that no one can come to Me unless it has been granted to him by My Father" (v. 65). He was referring to an earlier statement, recorded in verse 44: "No one can come to Me unless the Father who sent Me draws him." The implication was that wickedness and rebellion are so deeply ingrained in the character of fallen sinners that apart from divine grace, no one would ever believe.

Those were no doubt the final words many of them ever heard from Jesus. After all the miracles and gracious works they had seen Him do, this ought to have moved them to plead for grace, mercy, and new hearts. Instead, John says, "From that time many of His disciples went back and walked with Him no more" (v. 66). The verb tense means they ceased following Him permanently.

Jesus did not run after them with an explanation of what He really meant. He let the multitudes leave, then turned to the Twelve and said, "Do you also want to go away?" (v. 67). Peter, speaking as usual for the group, assured Him of their intention to stay on as disciples, and Jesus simply replied, "Did I not choose you, the twelve, and one of you is a devil?" (v. 70).

The Lord was not being pugnacious. He was being *truth-ful*—in a bold, clear way calculated to force them to declare whether or not they likewise loved the truth. He was asking true disciples to declare themselves, He was exposing the enmity of His antagonists, and He was forcing the halfhearted multitudes who were halting between two decisions to choose either one side or the other.

There were clearly aspects of the Pharisees' doctrine Jesus *could* have singled out to declare that He had some "common ground" with them. There was much positive energy in the initial eagerness of the crowds who followed Jesus. He might have harnessed that and doubled or tripled the size of His congregation.

He did not do that. He did the exact opposite—deliberately. Again, He was not interested in increasing the ranks of halfhearted disciples. His preaching had one aim: to declare truth, not to win accolades from the audience. For those who were not interested in hearing the truth, He did not try to make it easier to receive. What He did instead was make it impossible to ignore. People who heard Jesus preach could not walk away indifferent. Some left angry, some were deeply troubled by what He had to say, many had their eyes opened, and many more hardened their hearts against His message. Some became His disciples, and others became His adversaries. But no one who listened to Him preach for very long could possibly remain unchanged or apathetic.

I believe it to be a grave mistake to present Christianity as something charming and popular with no offence in it. Seeing that Christ went about the world giving the most violent offense to all kinds of people, it would seem absurd to expect that the doctrine of His person can be so presented as to offend nobody. We cannot blink at the fact that gentle Jesus, meek and mild, was so stiff in His opinions and so inflammatory in His language that He was thrown out of church, stoned, hunted from place to place, and finally gibbeted as a firebrand and a public danger. Whatever His peace was, it was not the peace of an amiable indifference.

—Dorothy Sayers

Seven

UNPARDONABLE SIN

Brood of vipers! How can you, being evil, speak good things?
For out of the abundance of the heart the mouth speaks.
MATTHEW 12:34

One other major turning point in Jesus' public dealings with the Jewish leaders must be mentioned. Some of the Pharisees who had been stalking Jesus suddenly went from accusing Him of blasphemy to committing an unpardonable blasphemy of their own. These religious experts, who were so outraged when Jesus declared a publican's sins instantly forgiven, were about to hear Him pronounce their sin *un*forgivable.

Jesus was being stalked by a group of Pharisees whose antagonism to Him knew no bounds. They continued to look for ways to discredit Him, but frankly, they had run out of arguments. It was absolutely clear to the multitudes that Jesus spoke for God, because there was no miracle He could not accomplish, no ailment He could not heal, and no argument from the Jewish leaders He could not answer.

Israel's religious elite were desperate. The apostle John describes a major council meeting in Jerusalem that took place either during this same phase of Jesus' ministry or shortly afterward. It gives us a window into how the Sanhedrin were thinking and what they were planning: "Then the chief priests and the Pharisees gathered a council and said, 'What shall we do? For this Man works many signs. If we let Him alone like this, everyone will believe in Him, and the Romans will come and take away both our place and nation'" (John 11:47–48).

Notice: they did not dispute the legitimacy of His claim that He was the Messiah or the reality of His miracles. They had no real argument against His doctrine, either—other than the fact that He represented a serious threat to their power.

In short, they feared the Romans more than they feared God. They wanted to hang on to the clout they had, rather than yield their honor and obedience to Israel's rightful Messiah. They loved their own artificial piety more than they craved authentic righteousness. They were satisfied with their own merits and contemptuous of anyone who questioned their godliness—as Jesus had done publicly and repeatedly.

Jesus' miracles made no impact on them whatsoever. They would not have thought differently about Him even if He had called down fire from heaven in their presence. They would not have liked Him any more if He had literally banished every last vestige of illness and suffering from the entire nation. They would have hated Him no matter what He did, as long as He refused to affirm and honor *them*. And He steadfastly refused to do that under any circumstances.

No wonder. Their own words reveal the evil in their hearts. They had all the evidence they needed in order to believe He was who He claimed to be. In fact, they were now convinced that if they simply "let Him alone like this, everyone [would soon] believe in Him" (John 11:48). They were determined to keep that from happening at all costs. They were already aggressively conspiring to kill Him. But that would take time. (The crucifixion was still at least a year away at this point.) In the meantime, the Pharisees would resort to whatever means they could to discredit or embarrass Him.

The Healing and Deliverance

The incident where Jesus pronounced them unforgivable was prompted by another indisputable miracle: "Then one was brought to Him who was demon-possessed, blind and mute; and He healed him, so that the blind and mute man both spoke and saw" (Matthew 12:22). The miracle was instantaneous, comprehensive, and triumphant on multiple levels. The man's physical disabilities were instantly healed, and he was freed from demonic bondage all at once.

Matthew says "multitudes" witnessed the miracle. Some of those people surely knew the man and his history, because the response to the healing was unusually strong. Of all the miracles they had seen, this one had a particular shock value—no doubt because the man's case was so severe. His blindness and inability to speak cut him off completely from all possible means of communication. That, combined with whatever grotesque manifestations his demonic possession might have caused, put him far beyond all earthly hope in the minds of everyone who knew him. But Jesus instantly made him completely well.

No one, including the Pharisees, could dispute the *fact* of the miracle. Immediately, a ripple of excitement went through the multitudes. They "were amazed and said, 'Could this be the Son of David?'" (v. 23). It was not an expression of doubt, nor was it a profession of faith. It was an exclamation of wonder and amazement. The miracle, on top of everything else they had seen and heard from Jesus, had them seriously pondering the possibility that He might indeed be the promised Messiah. He did not fit their expectations in most ways, because they were looking for the Messiah to explode on the scene as a conquering hero and glorious king, not as a simple carpenter's son from a family who lived in their midst. But they could not see so many dramatic miracles without beginning to wonder whether Jesus was indeed the One.

The Blasphemy

Hearing such talk surge through the multitudes, the Pharisees reacted quickly with the strongest denunciation of Jesus they could possibly put into words: "This fellow does not cast out demons except by Beelzebub, the ruler of the demons" (v. 24).

Beelzebub (or *Beelzebul*, as the better manuscripts have it) was a name borrowed and slightly altered from Baal-zebub (literally, "lord of the flies"), a deity of the Philistines (2 Kings 1:2–3, 6, 16). The alteration may have been deliberate, because *Beel-zebul* in Syriac means "god of dung." The name was used of Satan in Jesus' time. In other words, while the Pharisees could not deny that a bona fide miracle had occurred before their very eyes, they immediately began to insist that the power to perform the miracle came straight from Satan.

As usual, they muttered that charge in the midst of the multitude, out of earshot from Jesus. They were probably doing their best to discredit Him without catching His notice. They surely did not want another public confrontation. Every public clash they ever provoked with Him ended in embarrassment for them. They weren't bold enough to confront Jesus directly and make their charge to His face. But Matthew says:

> Jesus knew their thoughts, and said to them: "Every kingdom divided against itself is brought to desolation, and every city or house divided against itself will not stand. If Satan casts out Satan, he is divided against himself. How then will his kingdom stand? And if I cast out demons by Beelzebub, by whom do your sons cast them out? Therefore they shall be your judges. But if I cast out demons by the Spirit of God, surely the kingdom of God has come upon you."
>
> **(vv. 25–28)**

Surely by now you have noticed that Jesus' omniscience, particularly His ability to know what is going on in people's hearts, has been a consistent theme in His disputes with the Pharisees. John mentions it repeatedly (John 2:24–25; 6:64). Matthew mentions it here and in Matthew 9:4. Luke notes the same fact in an account that closely parallels this incident (Luke 11:17). If the stridency of Jesus' dealings with the Jewish leaders shocks you, bear in mind that He had the advantage of knowing their hearts even more perfectly than they themselves did. The fallen human heart is "deceitful above all things, and desperately wicked; who can know it?" (Jeremiah 17:9). The potential for self-deception is so profound that we are not to trust our own hearts (Proverbs 28:26). Only God knows how to judge a human heart perfectly (Jeremiah 11:20; 17:10; 20:12). Jesus *is* God, and therefore we can rest assured that His unrelenting harshness with the Pharisees was fully justified (Luke 16:15), even when He seemed to respond to them without much visible provocation.

Obviously you and I cannot assess other people's hearts perfectly—much less trust our own hearts (1 Samuel 16:7; John 7:24). Therefore we are also cautioned repeatedly to deal with others as patiently and as gently as possible (Galatians 6:1; Ephesians 4:2; Philippians 4:5; 2 Timothy 2:24–26).

Still, Jesus' constant friction with the Pharisees shows that conflict is sometimes necessary. Harsh words are not always inappropriate. Unpleasant and unwelcome truths sometimes need to be voiced. False religion always needs to be answered. Love may cover a multitude of sins (1 Peter 4:8), but the gross hypocrisy of false teachers desperately needs to be *un*covered— lest our silence facilitate and perpetuate a damning delusion. The truth is not always "nice."

In this case, Jesus took the Pharisees' murmured accusation, set it front and center before the whole multitude, and then deconstructed the logic of the charge. He pointed out first of all that a divided kingdom cannot stand. (Israel knew that fact all too well from her own history.) He noted that there were supposed exorcists among the Pharisees' disciples, and He raised the question of whose power *they* employed to cast out demons. The remark is tinged with sarcasm, because while there were exorcists in the Pharisees' system, they were notoriously unsuccessful—like the sons of Sceva ("a Jewish chief priest") mentioned in Acts 19:13–16, who tried using Jesus' name as an abracadabra to exorcise a demon-possessed man in Ephesus. Scripture says "the man in whom the evil spirit was leaped on them, overpowered them, and prevailed against them, so that they fled out of that house naked and wounded" (v. 16). So when Jesus challenged the Pharisees—"If I cast out demons by Beelzebub, by whom do your sons cast them out?" (Matthew 12:27)—it is not difficult to envision a wave of laughter moving through the watching crowd.

Given Jesus' one-hundred-percent success rate in casting out demons, the only reasonable and rational conclusion was that He was doing it by God's power—because only God is greater than the entire kingdom of Satan. "How can one enter a strong man's house and plunder his goods, unless he first binds the strong man? And then he will plunder his house" (v. 29).

Jesus' short reply to the Pharisees contained a couple of significant, ominous statements. He told them, for example, "If I cast out demons by the Spirit of God, surely the kingdom of God has come upon you" (v. 28). In other words, if they were wrong about Jesus (and they clearly were; even they knew so in their hearts), then He was indeed Israel's Messiah, and they were setting themselves against the power and authority of the kingdom of God in the very presence of the eternal King!

Furthermore, Jesus drew a stark line in the sand: "He who is not with Me is against Me" (v. 30). That statement, it appears, was mainly for the benefit of those in the multitude who were not fully committed disciples yet. They could not remain half-hearted and aloof while pretending to be His followers. By trying to sit on the fence between Jesus and the Pharisees, they were actually hardening their hearts against Christ. The proof that they were "against Him" would eventually be manifest in their own apostasy. Judas was the classic example of this. He had never once been overtly hostile to Jesus, until the day he betrayed Him for money. But that made it clear that Judas was never really "with" Jesus to begin with (cf. 1 John 2:19).

For the Pharisees who uttered the blasphemy, however, Jesus had even more solemn words.

Brood of Vipers!

If it seems Jesus was pronouncing a final judgment of damnation against these Pharisees right then and there, I believe that is precisely what He was doing. Having demonstrated the utter irrationality and irresponsibility of their accusation, he added this: "Therefore I say to you, every sin and blasphemy will be forgiven men, but the blasphemy against the Spirit will not be forgiven men. Anyone who speaks a word against the Son of Man, it will be forgiven him; but whoever speaks against the Holy Spirit, it will not be forgiven him, either in this age or in the age to come" (Matthew 12:31–32). Mark records the same statement in slightly different words: "Assuredly, I say to you, all sins will be forgiven the sons of men, and whatever blasphemies they may utter; but he who blasphemes against the Holy Spirit never has forgiveness, but is subject to eternal condemnation" (Mark 3:28–29). Mark adds this editorial comment, however: "because they said, 'He has an unclean spirit.'" (v. 30). Thus Mark makes it inescapably clear that Jesus' words about unpardonable sin were His response to the Pharisees' blasphemy. What is the unpardonable sin? What does Jesus mean when He speaks of the blasphemy against the Holy

Spirit? The context, as usual, gives a clear answer. It is the very blasphemy those men had just uttered.

The divine wrath that provoked those words of judgment is evident in the way He spoke to them: "Brood of vipers! How can you, being evil, speak good things? For out of the abundance of the heart the mouth speaks" (Matthew 12:34). The fruit of their own words demonstrated their true character (v. 33). Their condemnation was just.

Forgiveness and Unforgivability

People are often troubled by the notion that there is such a thing as unforgivable sin. Some worry about whether they might have inadvertently committed it. Some, noticing that Jesus did not elaborate a lot about the nature of the sin, try all kinds of hermeneutical gymnastics to define it as precisely as possible. Some have difficulty reconciling the notion of unpardonable sin with the doctrine of justification by faith and end up with a twisted idea of how salvation works. If it is possible to commit a blasphemy that can never be forgiven, they reason, then it must be possible for Christians to commit the sin and lose their salvation.

All those concerns and misunderstandings are easily answered, if we keep the context of this passage in view. These Pharisees were guilty of unpardonable sin because they knowingly—not in ignorance or by accident, but *deliberately*— wrote Jesus' work off as the work of the devil. Moreover, their rejection of Christ was a full, final, settled renunciation of Christ and everything He stood for. Contrast their sin with that of Peter, who later denied knowing Christ and punctuated his denials with swearing and curses. But Peter found forgiveness for his sin. If we think carefully about what was happening here and what Jesus actually said, the notion of unpardonable sin is not really so mysterious.

Notice, first of all, that this passage and its cross-references (Mark 3:28–29; Luke 12:10) are the only places where Scripture mentions unpardonable sin. Hebrews 6:4–6 and 10:26 describe a kind of willful apostasy for which there is no remedy, and 1 John 5:16 mentions "a sin unto death" (KJV). But the "sin unto death" is best understood as a sin that results in *physical* death. The New King James Version renders it accordingly: "sin leading to death." It is not one specific sin, but any sin whose direct consequence is death. The passages in Hebrews 6 and 10 describe a deliberate turning away from the truth. It is very similar to the blasphemy these Pharisees committed, and there may indeed be a legitimate correlation between those passages and the unpardonable sin. but the stress in Hebrews is on the impossibility of *repentance* (6:6), not the unobtainability of *forgiveness*.

Second, don't miss the fact that Jesus' words about this one unpardonable sin begin with a sweeping promise of forgiveness for "every sin and blasphemy" (Matthew 12:31). Our God is a forgiving God; that is His nature. "Who is a God like You, pardoning iniquity and passing over the transgression of the remnant of His heritage? He does not retain His anger forever, because He delights in mercy" (Micah 7:18). "For You, Lord, are good, and ready to forgive, and abundant in mercy to all those who call upon You" (Psalm 86:5). Scripture is full of texts like those.

Jesus emphatically states that the *severity* of sin never hinders God's forgiveness. "All manner of sin and blasphemy" is forgivable (Matthew 12:31 KJV). After all, the grossest sin ever committed was the crucifixion of Jesus (Acts 2:23), and yet one of Jesus' last sayings before He died was a prayer for forgiveness for His executioners and the crowd who mocked Him (Luke 23:34). The *number* of sins a person commits does not make his case unpardonable. The redemption purchased by Christ will "cover a multitude of sins" (James 5:20). The *species* of sin isn't the factor that makes it unpardonable. "If we confess our sins, He is faithful and just to forgive us our sins and to cleanse us from *all* unrighteousness" (1 John 1:9). Over the course of His ministry, Jesus forgave every conceivable kind and category of wickedness. Even as He hung on the cross, He granted full and immediate pardon to a thief who had lived a full life of sin—because the man was truly repentant.

Here, then, was the issue with the Pharisees. Their hatred for Jesus was fixed and utterly immovable. They would never repent, and their blasphemy simply demonstrated beyond doubt how inexorably hardened their hearts had become. In the face of a miracle that completely shocked and amazed all who saw it, they were concerned only with how to discredit Christ.

Not only were their hearts permanently hardened against Christ; they were fully resolved to do everything possible to turn as many others as possible against Him. Their hatred for Him was driven by murderous intentions, and now it was compounded with the ultimate blasphemy.

Notice that He refers to the unpardonable sin as *"the* blasphemy against the Spirit" (Matthew 12:31). The definite article is significant. Jesus clearly was speaking about one particular act of blasphemy—the ultimate, conclusive, in-your-face expression of blasphemy that rises above all other forms of blasphemy. He was not suggesting that a slip of the tongue invoking the Holy Spirit's name in a blasphemous oath is automatically unpardonable. He was dealing with one very specific exhibition of gross blasphemy, and *that* is what He said was unforgivable. It was the sin of those Pharisees: closing one's heart permanently against Christ even after the Holy Spirit has brought full conviction of the truth. In effect, Jesus closed the door of heaven against these Pharisees who had so utterly and deliberately shut their hearts against Him.

Why did He characterize their sin as blasphemy against *the Holy Spirit*? Because Jesus' miracles were done in the power of the Holy Spirit. (Even the Pharisees knew that in their hearts.) And yet they claimed He was operating in Satan's power. In effect, they were calling the Holy Spirit the devil, and giving the devil credit for what the Spirit of God had done.

But what made this particular sin unpardonable was the finality of it. It was deliberate. It was an expression of cold-hearted, determined unbelief. These Pharisees had seen, up close, more evidence than they could possibly ever need that Jesus was God incarnate. And yet they continued to press for more dramatic signs. In fact, right after Jesus admonished them about the danger of unpardonable sin, they demanded another sign—suggesting that they wanted to see a sign of cosmic proportions (v. 38)—"A sign from heaven," in the words of Luke 11:16.

The fact is, their hearts were already settled. They would never believe, no matter what Jesus ever did or said. Therefore their sin was unforgivable.

Immediately after that day, Jesus began to teach in parables (Matthew 13:3). From that day forward, when He taught in public settings, "Jesus spoke to the multitude in parables; and without a parable He did not speak to them" (v. 34). That was at least in part an expression of judgment against the hardheartedness of the Pharisees. Quoting from Isaiah 6:9–10 and 44:18, Jesus explained to His disciples the reason for the parables: "To you it has been given to know the mystery of the kingdom of God; but to those who are outside, all things come in parables, so that 'seeing they may see and not perceive, and hearing they may hear and not understand; lest they should turn, and their sins be forgiven them'" (Mark 4:11–12). If Israel's religious elite were so determined to reject the truth, He would conceal the truth from them with parables, while using those same parables to illustrate the truth for His disciples. And "when they were alone, He explained all things to His disciples" (v. 34).

But the parables also served a *merciful* purpose in Jesus' dealings with the Pharisees. With their hearts now permanently hardened against the truth, the more truth they heard, the greater their final judgment would be. Because their determination to oppose the truth was now permanent and final, the less truth they heard from Jesus, the better it would be for them.

The Pharisees' pattern of antagonism toward Jesus continued unabated and in fact dramatically increased. Luke 20:20 says, "They watched Him, and sent spies who pretended to be righteous, that they might seize on His words, in order to deliver Him to the power and the authority of the governor." They continually put Him to the test (Matthew 22:15, 35; Mark 12:13; Luke 11:54), and they repeatedly embarrassed themselves in the process. Every subsequent encounter He had with them was more of the same.

Jesus always withstood them, and He invariably silenced them. He often warned His disciples about the tendencies of the Pharisees' system, referring to their hypocrisy as "leaven" (Matthew 16:6; Luke 12:1). But He had little else to say *to* them other than the same truths they had already heard from Him.

In the end, during that final week before the crucifixion, He would sum up His views about Israel's religious leaders and their hypocrisy in a scalding diatribe in their front yard—the temple grounds in Jerusalem. That sermon would leave them fuming and outraged, and it would seal their determination to kill Him as soon as they possibly could.

We have all heard people say a hundred times over, for they seem never to tire of saying it, that the Jesus of the New Testament is indeed a most merciful and humane lover of humanity, but that the Church has hidden this human character in repellent dogmas and stiffened it with ecclesiastical terrors till it has taken on an inhuman character. This is, I venture to repeat, very nearly the reverse of the truth. The truth is that it is the image of Christ in the churches that is almost entirely mild and merciful.

—G. K. Chesterton

Eight

WOE

Woe to you, scribes and Pharisees, hypocrites! For you are like whitewashed tombs which indeed appear beautiful outwardly, but inside are full of dead men's bones and all uncleanness. See! Your house is left to you desolate.
MATTHEW 23:27, 38

All of Matthew 23 is the record of one sermon. It is the last public sermon Jesus ever preached. Its subject matter is not the gospel or the kingdom of God *per se;* it is a powerful onslaught of rebuke against the religious sins of Israel, and her leaders in particular. How ironic (and how supremely significant) it is that the One of whom it was said, "God did not send His Son into the world to condemn the world, but that the world through Him might be saved" (John 3:17) made His last public sermon an extended message of condemnation.

It was the middle of Passion Week. The events of that tumultuous week began with Jesus entering Jerusalem on the back of a donkey with shouts of "Hosanna!" reverberating through the city. It looked for all the world as if He would be swept on a massive wave of public support into prominence and power in some political capacity—and then He would finally inaugurate His promised kingdom. But the public's enthusiasm for Christ was an illusion.

Jerusalem was happy to have a worker of miracles and the hope of a conquering King. But they did not want Jesus' hard preaching. They were shocked that He seemed more interested in challenging their religious institutions than He was in conquering Rome and liberating them from political oppression. They were stunned by His treatment of Israel's religious elite. He spent more time calling *Israel* to repentance than He did criticizing her oppressors. On top of that, they did not appreciate His refusal to be Messiah on *their* terms (John 6:15). Before the week was over, some of the same people who praised Him with hosannas would be screaming for His blood.

Not in My Father's House

On Tuesday morning of that fateful week, Jesus repeated the cleansing of the temple. Almost exactly three years had elapsed since He first came on the scene as a prophet with a whip of cords, chasing the unscrupulous animal merchants and money changers from the temple. Back then, it seemed as if He stormed into the temple compound out of nowhere, and He took the religious authorities completely by surprise. It was clear they did not know what to do with Him.

Now, three years later, the profiteering money changers were back on the job, as were the unscrupulous animal sellers. Not much had changed, except that the Jewish leaders' hearts had grown harder and colder—and now they knew exactly what they wanted to do with Jesus.

Mark gives the fullest account:

> Jesus went into the temple and began to drive out those who bought and sold in the temple, and overturned the tables of the money changers and the seats of those who sold doves. And He would not allow anyone to carry wares through the temple. Then He taught, saying to them, "Is it not written, 'My house shall be called a house of prayer for all nations'? But you have made it a 'den of thieves.'" And the scribes and chief priests heard it and sought how they might destroy Him; for they feared Him, because all the people were astonished at His teaching.
>
> **(Mark 11:15–18)**

It makes perfect sense that Jesus would conclude His ministry by making the very same point He made at the outset. The idea that He cleansed the temple twice does not strain common sense or credulity in the least. What is truly remarkable is that Jesus did not do this every time He visited Jerusalem over the course of His ministry. He did it just once at the beginning and then again at the end, bracketing His public ministry.

These dramatic public displays of Jesus' divine authority highlight His opposition to the religious institutions of apostate Judaism. They stress the prophetic nature of His message and explain to a large degree why His interactions with the Jewish leaders were always heavily flavored with gall.

By now, the rank-and-file members of the Sanhedrin, the Pharisees, the chief priests, the leading Sadducees, and the temple guard all hated Him more than ever. But they also still feared Him (Mark 11:18)—mainly because He seemed so popular with the people. So instead of arresting Him then and there on the temple grounds, their plan was to lie in wait for an opportunity to arrest Him in secret. That's why this time Jesus was able to drive the money changers from the temple and walk away from the scene totally unchallenged. The first time Jesus drove out the money changers, the temple guard responded by demanding that He give a sign that would prove His prophetic authority. This time, their response was just mute amazement. And while they remained largely in the background, the Sanhedrin quietly renewed their resolve to get rid of Him—that very week, if possible.

For His part, immediately after driving out the money changers, Jesus more or less moved into the temple grounds for the week. The temple courts became both classroom and headquarters for His public teaching ministry, right under the Sanhedrin's nose. Most of Matthew 21–25; Mark 11–13; Luke 19–21, and John 12 record what He taught and things that happened there during that week. The religious leaders repeatedly challenged Him, trying to trap Him or confound Him some way—and they always failed. Luke says, "He was teaching daily in the temple. But the chief priests, the scribes, and the leaders of the people sought to destroy Him, and were unable to do anything; for all the people were very attentive to hear Him" (Luke 19:47–48).

John adds this foreboding note about the crowds who listened to Jesus' teaching that week: "But although He had done so many signs before them, they did not believe in Him" (John 12:37).

Making an Impact

Someone might wonder why Jesus continued teaching in the temple courts when He knew the hearts of so many of His hearers were dull and cold. After all, stirring up strife like this could not possibly do anyone any good, could it?

But as always, the truth mattered more to Jesus than how people felt about it. He wasn't looking for ways to make people "like" Him; He was calling people who were willing to bow to Him unconditionally as their Lord. He wasn't interested in reinforcing the "common-ground" beliefs where His message overlapped with the Pharisees' worldview. On the contrary, He stressed (almost exclusively) the points on which He *disagreed* with them. His strategy frankly would not have been any more welcome in the typical twenty-first-century evangelical gathering than it was right there in the Sanhedrin's backyard.

And yet, in modest but significant ways, Jesus was making an impact. John 12:42–43, describing Jesus' ministry that week in the temple courtyard, says this: "Nevertheless even among the rulers many believed in Him, but because of the Pharisees they did not confess Him, lest they should be put out of the synagogue; for they loved the praise of men more than the praise of God." Evidently, Nicodemus and Joseph of Arimathea were representative of a small, quiet, almost invisible group of council members and influential rabbis who listened to Jesus and were persuaded of the truth of His message. Because love for the praise of men was so deeply ingrained in their worldview, they kept silent.

Among the common people, spurious faith and halfhearted Messianic hope in Jesus was likewise a significant problem. It always had been. Remember that John drew attention to the problem at the very start, in John 2:23–24: "Many believed in His name when they saw the signs . . . but Jesus did not commit Himself to them, because He knew all men." John 6 described in detail how such halfhearted faith so quickly gave way to hostility. It was about to happen again. Regarding those appreciative crowds who listened to Jesus eagerly during that final week in Jerusalem, "hanging on to every word He said" (Luke 19:48 NASB)—there must have been countless numbers of them who would be chanting "Crucify Him!" (Mark 15:13) before the week was over.

And yet there was a remnant in both groups—the Jewish leaders and the common people—who either were or would become true disciples. Jesus kept preaching for their benefit, even though He knew full well that the more visible He made His ministry in the public eye, the more the Sanhedrin's resolve to crucify Him intensified.

The Final Sermon

The content of Jesus' message demonstrates, however, that He was teaching not only for the benefit of the believing remnant, but also as a final warning and instruction to the Jewish leaders themselves.

Our Lord's last public sermon took place on Wednesday of that final week. Matthew 23:1 says He delivered His message "to the crowds and to His disciples" (NASB). But it is clear from the message itself that members of the council were among the bystanders, because Jesus called them out and addressed major portions of the sermon directly to them. They were not only standing on the perimeter as usual, but actually mixing in with the crowds incognito, and pretending to be sympathetic hearers. They were listening carefully for anything they might use to "trap Him in what He said" (22:15 NASB) or to twist into an accusation against Him. Here is where Luke says,

> And the chief priests and the scribes that very hour sought to lay hands on Him, but they feared the people—for they knew He had spoken this parable against them. So they watched Him, and sent spies who pretended to be righteous, that they might seize on His words, in order to deliver Him to the power and the authority of the governor.
>
> (Luke 20:19–20)

Of course, Jesus *still* knew their thoughts, and He confronted them more directly than ever before. He used some of the sharpest language He ever employed. He called them names. He let loose with waves of condemnation against their hypocrisy, their Scripture-twisting, and their self-righteousness. He pronounced woe after woe against them. And the expression "woe" was no mild imprecation; it was the strongest conceivable prophetic curse. And you can be certain its meaning was not lost on them.

How to Lose Friends and Inflame Enemies

From His opening words to His final sentence, Jesus was stern, candid, passionate, and intense—even fierce. As always, He told them what they most needed to hear, declaring the truth to them in unvarnished language. The tenor of His words reminds us that spiritual warfare is just that: a battle.

It is significant that Jesus, who as omniscient God incarnate, was the most sensitive Person ever to walk the earth, and yet in circumstances like these, He refused to tone down the message, adopt a delicate tone, or handle His spiritual adversaries as fragile souls. Too much was at stake.

He began the message in a comparatively low-key fashion, mocking the Pharisees' proud self-righteousness and calling His followers to be as humble as the Pharisees were arrogant:

> The scribes and the Pharisees sit in Moses' seat. Therefore whatever they tell you to observe, that observe and do, but do not do according to their works; for they say, and do not do. For they bind heavy burdens, hard to bear, and lay them on men's shoulders; but they themselves will not move them with one of their fingers. But all their works they do to be seen by men. They make their phylacteries broad and enlarge the borders of their garments. They love the best places at feasts, the best seats in the synagogues, greetings in the marketplaces, and to be called by men, "Rabbi, Rabbi." But you, do not be called "Rabbi"; for One is your Teacher, the Christ, and you are all brethren. Do not call anyone on earth your father; for One is your Father, He who is in heaven. And do not be called teachers; for One is your Teacher, the Christ. But he who is greatest

among you shall be your servant. And whoever exalts himself will be humbled, and he who humbles himself will be exalted.

(Matthew 23:2–12)

Notice that Jesus said, "Whatever they tell you to observe, that observe and do, but do not do according to their works" (v. 3). The Pharisees were not wrong in *everything* they taught. It would be a total misapplication of Jesus' teaching to take His condemnation of Pharisee religion and conclude that He endorsed whatever seemed to be the opposite of what they advocated. In their emphasis on the authority and gravity of the law, especially as it governed public morality, they were generally right. When it came to those issues, what Jesus abhorred about them was not what they said people should or shouldn't do; it was their failure to live in accord with their own teaching. That was the great danger posed by their obsession with externals. They paid careful attention to what they wore, but not so much to what they thought about. They were deeply concerned with how they were perceived by other people but not so concerned with what God thought of them. They were passionate about making sure *they* received earthly honor, but they hardly cared about God's honor. *Don't be like them* was the starting point of the whole sermon.

Then Jesus spoke directly to the scribes and Pharisees who were there: "But woe to you, scribes and Pharisees, hypocrites!" (v. 13). And thus He launched into a diatribe against them that consumes the rest of the chapter. From that point to the end of the message, Jesus speaks directly to the Jewish leaders in second person—His most blistering attack on them to date.

139

The sermon is much too long to analyze word for word, but it is worth reading the entire portion that was addressed directly to Israel's religious elite:

But woe to you, scribes and Pharisees, hypocrites! For you shut up the kingdom of heaven against men; for you neither go in yourselves, nor do you allow those who are entering to go in. Woe to you, scribes and Pharisees, hypocrites! For you devour widows' houses, and for a pretense make long prayers. Therefore you will receive greater condemnation.

Woe to you, scribes and Pharisees, hypocrites! For you travel land and sea to win one proselyte, and when he is won, you make him twice as much a son of hell as yourselves.

Woe to you, blind guides, who say, "Whoever swears by the temple, it is nothing; but whoever swears by the gold of the temple, he is obliged to perform it." Fools and blind! For which is greater, the gold or the temple that sanctifies the gold? And, "Whoever swears by the altar, it is nothing; but whoever swears by the gift that is on it, he is obliged to perform it." Fools and blind! For which is greater, the gift or the altar that sanctifies the gift? Therefore he who swears by the altar, swears by it and by all things on it. He who swears by the temple, swears by it and by Him who dwells in it. And he who swears by heaven, swears by the throne of God and by Him who sits on it.

Woe to you, scribes and Pharisees, hypocrites! For you pay tithe of mint and anise and cummin, and have neglected the weightier matters of the law: justice and mercy and faith. These you ought to have done, without leaving the others undone. Blind guides, who strain out a gnat and swallow a camel!

Woe to you, scribes and Pharisees, hypocrites! For you cleanse the outside of the cup and dish, but inside they are full of extortion and self-indulgence. Blind Pharisee, first cleanse the inside of the cup and dish, that the outside of them may be clean also.

Woe to you, scribes and Pharisees, hypocrites! For you are like whitewashed tombs which indeed appear beautiful outwardly, but inside are full of dead men's bones and all uncleanness. Even so you also outwardly appear righteous to men, but inside you are full of hypocrisy and lawlessness.

Woe to you, scribes and Pharisees, hypocrites! Because you build the tombs of the prophets and adorn the monuments of the righteous, and say, "If we had lived in the days of our fathers, we would not have been partakers with them in the blood of the prophets."

Therefore you are witnesses against yourselves that you are sons of those who murdered the prophets. Fill up, then, the measure of your fathers' guilt. Serpents, brood of vipers! How can you escape the condemnation of hell? Therefore, indeed, I send you prophets, wise men, and scribes: some of them you will kill and crucify, and some of them you will scourge in your synagogues and persecute from city to city, that on you may come all the righteous blood shed on the earth, from the blood of righteous Abel to the blood of Zechariah, son of Berechiah, whom you murdered between the temple and the altar. Assuredly, I say to you, all these things will come upon this generation.

O Jerusalem, Jerusalem, the one who kills the prophets and stones those who are sent to her! How often I wanted to gather your children together, as a hen gathers her chicks under her wings, but you were not willing! See! Your house is left to you desolate; for I say to you, you shall see Me no more till you say, "Blessed is He who comes in the name of the LORD!"

(vv. 13–39)

Jesus had said many of those same things before. Once a private lunch meeting in a Pharisee's home had dissolved into a conflict when it became obvious that He had been invited mainly so that they could observe and criticize things like His failure to observe their ceremonial washings. On that occasion, in the presence of several Pharisees, Jesus delivered a scathing tongue-lashing in which He said many of these same things (Luke 11:37–54). But this was the first time where it is recorded that Jesus had made such a sustained attack on official Judaism publicly—in Jerusalem, at the temple, no less.

Eight times He pronounces *woe* against them. Remember that the Sermon on the Mount began with eight beatitudes. These pronouncements of woe are the polar opposite of those, and they stand in stark contrast. These are curses rather than blessings.

And yet even in the curses, there is a poignancy that reflects Jesus' sorrow. He is not expressing a *preference* for their condemnation, because, after all, He came to save, not to condemn (John 3:17). Nevertheless, Jesus' profound sorrow over the hardhearted rebellion of the Pharisees did not move Him to mute His message or soft-sell the reality of the spiritual calamity they had brought upon themselves. If anything, that was why He delivered this final message to them with such passion and urgency.

The other word that dominates this sermon besides *woe* is *hypocrites*—which likewise appears eight times. In the course of pronouncing those eight woes, Jesus was addressing many of the doctrinal and practical errors that illustrated what deplorable hypocrites they were. These included their pretentious praying (v. 14); their misguided motives for "ministry" to others (v. 15); their tendency to swear casually by things that are holy, plus the corresponding habit of playing fast and loose with their vows (vv. 18–22); their upside-down approach to priorities, by which they had elevated obscure ceremonial precepts over the moral law (vv. 23–24); and above all, their blithe toleration of many gross, often ludicrous, manifestations of hypocrisy (vv. 27–31).

One other characteristic that makes this sermon stand out is Jesus' liberal use of derogatory epithets. Those who think name-calling is inherently un-Christlike and always inappropriate will have a very hard time with this sermon. In addition to the eight times Jesus emphatically calls them "hypocrites!" He calls them "blind guides" (vv. 16, 24); "fools and blind!" (v. 17, 19); "blind Pharisee[s]" (v. 26); and "serpents, brood of vipers!" (v. 33).

This was not an attempt to win esteem in their eyes. He wasn't trying to persuade them with smooth words or a friendly overture. These were not soft words designed to turn away wrath.

But it was *truth,* and that is what the Pharisees and all who had been influenced by them desperately needed to hear.

Not So Meek and Mild

Sadly, this sermon was also a pronouncement of final judgment against the religious leaders and their followers who had rejected Christ and who by now had so hardened their hearts against Him that they would never believe. It underscored in a verbally graphic way the finality of the judgment Jesus had rendered when He pronounced the Pharisees' blasphemy unpardonable. It also effectively expanded that judgment to include not only other hardened unbelievers, but also the institutions that had become monuments to that corrupt religious system—the Sanhedrin, the corrupt priesthood, the Pharisees and Sadducees—the whole religious hierarchy that had in effect taken over the temple.

At the end of the message, when Jesus said, "See! Your house is left to you desolate" (v. 38), He was pronouncing *Ichabod* ("the glory has departed") on the temple. Instead of "My Father's house" (John 2:16), it was now "your house." The Glory of Israel departed the temple for good, not to return again until all Israel says, "Blessed is He who comes in the name of the Lord!"

Before that generation passed from the scene, Roman armies laid waste to Herod's temple. From then until now, Israel has had no temple, no sacrifices, no means of fulfilling the most important aspects of their ceremonial law, no other means of atonement apart from the Lamb of God who took away the sin of the world. Thus His dramatic departure from the temple was a major turning point for all Israel.

No wonder He spoke with such passion and intensity.

We can learn a lot from observing how Jesus dealt with false religion and its purveyors. Those who set themselves up as teachers representing the Lord and influencing others while corrupting the truth need to be denounced and refuted—for their sake, for the sake of others who are victimized by their errors, and especially for the glory of Christ, who *is* Truth incarnate.

ABOUT THE AUTHOR

John MacArthur is the pastor-teacher of Grace Community Church in Sun Valley, California, as well as an author, conference speaker, chancellor emeritus of The Master's University and Seminary, and featured teacher with the Grace to You media ministry.

After graduating from Talbot Theological Seminary, John came to Grace Community Church in 1969. The emphasis of his pulpit ministry is the careful study and verse-by-verse exposition of the Bible, with special attention devoted to the historical and grammatical background behind each passage. Under John's leadership, Grace Community Church's congregation has expanded to several thousand members, who participate every week in dozens of fellowship groups and training programs, most led by lay leaders and each dedicated to equipping members for ministry on local, national, and international levels.

In 1985, John became president of The Master's College (formerly Los Angeles Baptist College; since 2016, The Master's University). Located in Santa Clarita, California, it is a distinctly Christian, accredited, liberal arts institution offering undergraduate and graduate degree programs. In 1986, John founded The Master's Seminary, a graduate school dedicated to training men for full-time pastoral and missionary work.

John is also chairman and featured teacher with Grace to You. Founded in 1969, Grace to You is the nonprofit organization responsible for developing, producing, and distributing John's books, audio resources, and the *Grace to You* radio and television programs. *Grace to You* radio airs more than a thousand times daily throughout the English-speaking world, reaching major population centers with biblical truth. It also airs over a thousand times a day in Spanish, reaching twenty-seven countries across Europe and Latin America. *Grace to You* television airs weekly on DirecTV in the United States, and is available for free on the Internet worldwide. John's 3,300-plus sermons, spanning more than five decades of ministry, are available for free download on this website.

John has written hundreds of study guides and books, including *The Gospel According to Jesus*, *Our Sufficiency in Christ*, *Strange Fire*, *Ashamed of the Gospel*, *The Murder of Jesus*, *The Prodigal Son*, *Twelve Ordinary Men*, *The Truth War*, *The Jesus You Can't Ignore*, *Slave*, *One Perfect Life*, *The Gospel According to Paul*, *Parables*, and *One Faithful Life*. John's books have been translated into more than two dozen languages. *The MacArthur Study Bible*, the cornerstone resource of his ministry, is available in English (NKJV, NASB, and ESV), Spanish, Russian, German, French, Portuguese, Italian, Arabic, and Chinese.

In 2015 The MacArthur New Testament Commentary series was completed. In thirty-four volumes, John takes you detail by detail, verse by verse, through the entire New Testament.

John and his wife, Patricia, live in Southern California and have four married children: Matt, Marcy, Mark, and Melinda. They also enjoy the enthusiastic company of their fifteen grandchildren.